William Arnold Stevens, Alvah Hovey, Ezra Palmer Gould

Commentary on the epistle to the Philippians

Vol. 4

William Arnold Stevens, Alvah Hovey, Ezra Palmer Gould

Commentary on the epistle to the Philippians
Vol. 4

ISBN/EAN: 9783337731052

Printed in Europe, USA, Canada, Australia, Japan

Cover: Foto ©Lupo / pixelio.de

More available books at **www.hansebooks.com**

AN

AMERICAN COMMENTARY

ON THE

NEW TESTAMENT.

EDITED BY

ALVAH HOVEY, D.D., LL.D.

PHILADELPHIA.
AMERICAN BAPTIST PUBLICATION SOCIETY,
1420 CHESTNUT STREET.

ON THE

EPISTLE TO THE PHILIPPIANS.

BY

J. B. GOUGH PIDGE, D. D.

PHILADELPHIA:
AMERICAN BAPTIST PUBLICATION SOCIETY,
1420 CHESTNUT STREET.

INTRODUCTION TO THE EPISTLE TO THE PHILIPPIANS.

It was a decisive moment in the missionary career of the Apostle Paul, when, summoned by the vision of a man of Macedonia, he sailed from Troas, and crossing the Ægean Sea, set foot for the first time upon the soil of Europe. Immediately before him as he landed lay the important city of Philippi, which in earlier times had been called Crenides, or fountains, on account of its numerous springs, but was afterward named Philippi in honor of the great Macedonian conqueror who had enlarged and fortified it. From its vicinity to the field of the battle which ended the Roman republic, between Octavius and Antony on the one side, and Brutus and Cassius on the other, it had become a famous historical landmark, and as a Roman colony with the so-called *jus Italicum*, or privilege of Roman citizenship, it outranked all the other cities of Macedonia. But its highest glory was conferred upon it when Paul entered its gates bearing the message of salvation, and it became the first city of Europe to listen to the gospel from the lips of an apostle.

Paul's first stay in Philippi was very brief, owing to the treatment he received at the hands of the Roman magistrates (Acts 16 : 16–40), but he left behind a most important result of his short visit in a little band of converts who formed the nucleus of a most remarkable church. On at least two subsequent occasions Paul revisited the place (Acts 20 : 2, 6), most likely making somewhat longer visits than on the first occasion, and possibly he made still another visit after his release from his first Roman imprisonment. The members of the church which he founded there must have consisted chiefly of heathen converts, since there appears to have been but a small number of Jews residing in Philippi. At the time of his first visit we find mostly women, meeting for prayer by the river side (Acts 16 : 13), the fact that they possessed no synagogue showing how few in numbers and how poor they were. Between this Philippian Church and the great apostle the most friendly and cordial relations existed from first to last. It was the only church under his charge that never gave him occasion for rebuke or reproof. Its members were never seduced from their steadfast loyalty to him and to his teachings, nor did they ever fall into any such terrible sins as appeared elsewhere, or give heed to doctrinal errors, as even the neighboring church of Thessalonica seems to have done. In the letter before us Paul declares that he had never had occasion for anything but joy and gratitude in all his remembrance of them. From the first day they had maintained with him and with each other the closest kind of fellowship. A slight ripple had indeed been excited in the otherwise calm current of their spiritual life by the dissensions of two women of influence, but beyond this nothing had occurred to give the apostle the least anxiety in regard to their unity and harmony. Of course, the same dangers threatened them, that threatened the other apostolic churches,—dangers from persecuting heathen, from false Jewish teachers, and from the pernicious example of worldly Christians. Against all these threatening perils the apostle urges them to stand fast in a spirit of loving, unselfish harmony, and of careful observance both of his teachings and life. While Paul himself declares that they had always been obedient, we find no hint in subsequent literature of any deviation from this high standard of loyal and steadfast obedience.

The Philippian Church revealed its lovely and unselfish character especially in its treatment of the apostle's personal needs, a sort of consideration he seems never to have received at the hands of any other church. While he was still in Macedonia, in the neighboring city of Thessalonica, soon after his first visit to Philippi, they kindly sent supplies to relieve his necessities more than once. At a later period they were for a long time unable to do anything for him,—though their hearts were always ready,—until the visit of Epaphroditus to Rome furnished them with the long-coveted opportunity. Then their old spirit, like a tree in spring time, blossomed out again in a most loving and lavish contribution to his needs, that awakened all the deepest feelings of the apostle's tender heart, and gave occasion for this letter in return. It was apparently entrusted to the same messenger, who had brought their gifts, and who had deepened and intensified the apostle's sense of gratitude by carrying out his mission in such a self-sacrificing spirit as to bring upon himself a dangerous and almost fatal sickness, which led the apostle to send him back to Philippi sooner than he would otherwise have done.

As the Epistle was not called forth, like most of the others that Paul wrote, by any doctrinal or practical danger threatening the church, it is written in an entirely different tone and style from any of his other writings. It is not divided, as the rest are, into two portions, one pre-eminently doctrinal, the other pre-eminently practical and hortatory; but the thought flows on from beginning to end in a most unstudied and natural way, like an ordinary friendly letter. There is, of course, a certain order of thought, but there are no rigid and clearly marked divisions between the different portions In a free and natural way the apostle touches upon four special topics; first, his own condition and prospects; second, the necessity for unity and steadfastness on the part of the church; third, the threatening dangers from Judaizing teachers; and fourth, the special subject of the contribution which he has received from the church. This is the outline in general of the order of thought; the more minute analysis is as follows:

After the usual address and salutation (1 : 1, 2), the apostle gratefully recognizes the favorable condition of the church at Philippi, and prays that it may develop more and more richly in all the essentials of Christian life. (1 : 3-11.) He briefly describes his condition and labors at Rome, revealing at the same time his exalted state of mind amid the uncertainties and dangers of his position (1 : 12-26), and exhorts his brethren to unity, humility, and steadfastness in view of the inspiring example of Jesus Christ the Lord. (1 : 27-2 : 11.) This line of exhortation leads to the noble doctrinal passage describing Christ's condescension, humiliation, and subsequent exaltation (2 : 5-11), when the practical tone is again resumed, and the Philippians are urged to work out their salvation in such a spirit as to make them bright examples in the midst of a wicked world (2 : 12-18); after which the apostle speaks very feelingly of the spirit and labors of his messengers and assistants, Timothy (2 : 19-24) and Epaphroditus. (2 : 25-30.) Apparently about to close his Epistle, Paul is led by some unknown occasion to the thought of his Jewish opponents, and he launches out into an indignant contrast between their example and his own, earnestly admonishes the Philippians to imitate him rather than them (3 : 1-16), and draws a vivid picture of the contrasted character and destiny of true and false believers. (3 : 17-4 : 1.) Admonitions, mixed with commendations, addressed to individuals (4 : 2, 3), general exhortations to joyfulness and spiritual mindedness (4 : 4-9), followed by a most beautiful and delicate recognition of the kindness of the church in their gifts (4 : 10–20), with salutations and a benediction (4 : 21–23), conclude the Epistle.

We assign the Epistle to the time of Paul's imprisonment in Rome in accordance with universal tradition, the indications of the letter itself, and the views of nearly all commentators. It may be well, however, to mention the highly improbable opinion that it was written at Cesarea during the period of Paul's imprisonment there. In favor of this view are cited the facts, that Paul was in prison at the time, in a place called the Prætorium (Acts 23 : 35, same word), and among Roman soldiers; but all of these facts agree equally well with the theory of its composition at Rome, while there are many features of his condition and the state of affairs around him revealed in this Epistle, which are not so easily reconciled with the Cesarean, as with the Roman imprisonment; for instance, the widespread influence of his example, of which there is no hint in Luke's account of the stay at Cesarea, but which fully accords with the description of his residence at Rome (Acts 28 : see especially ver. 30, 31); the large number of brethren who were affected in various ways toward him, implying a large city; his uncertainty as to the event of his trial, which he would much more probably have felt at Rome, where his trial was impending, than at Cesarea, where it was still remote; and finally and most decisively his allusion to "Cæsar's household." (4 : 22.) We therefore assume the place of composition to be Rome, and the time to be toward the close of Paul's first imprisonment, A. D. 63 or 64, which we infer from the fact that the apostle has evidently been a long time in prison, and looks forward to a speedy decision of his case. This was therefore most probably the last epistle which was written by Paul to any church. And surely the great apostle to the Gentiles could have closed this marvelous series of inspired letters to the churches he had founded, with nothing more beautiful and appropriate than this loving and tender Epistle, which expresses so ardently his perfect joy and gratitude over the remarkable fellowship of this beloved church, exhibits so gloriously his calm and heroic spirit of resignation and triumph in view of a possible martyrdom, and accepts so delicately and graciously the material gifts of his brethren, even as a noble king might receive the offerings of devoted subjects. This is indeed an Epistle of the heart, and so a most fitting close to the series of Epistles which the great-hearted Paul wrote to the churches.

THE EPISTLE TO THE PHILIPPIANS.

CHAPTER I.

PAUL and Timotheus, the servants of Jesus Christ, to all the saints in Christ Jesus which are at Philippi, with the bishops and deacons:	1 Paul and Timothy, [1]servants of Christ Jesus, to all the saints in Christ Jesus who are at Philippi, with

1 Or, *bondservants.*

Ch. 1 : 1, 2. ADDRESS AND SALUTATION.

1. Paul and Timotheus. Paul begins his Epistle with a brief but comprehensive greeting. In harmony with the friendly tone of the entire letter, he makes no allusion to his apostolic dignity, but affectionately associating his fellow-laborer Timothy with himself, sends a greeting in their united name to the church. The mention of Timothy may have been caused by the apostle's desire to secure a favorable reception for him on the visit he was purposing soon to make, by revealing his own high estimate of that disciple's character. Besides, Timothy was already well known to the Philippians from previous visits, and so a greeting might appropriately be sent from him as well as the apostle. Whether he was Paul's amanuensis in the writing of the letter or not, we have no means of deciding.

The servants of Jesus Christ. As his apostolic claims had not been assailed in Philippi, Paul had no occasion to assert them, and therefore adopts the lowly title of servant,[1] to which his natural modesty inclines him. He belongs to Christ as his master, a fact of which he never loses sight, not even in those epistles where he asserts and vindicates his apostolic dignity. Paul omits his official designation only in this Epistle, the two to the Thessalonians, and that to Philemon. As to his personal name, it is to be noted that he invariably uses his Greek name Paul, and not his Hebrew name Saul, in all his epistles. We suppose this was due to the fact that these letters were all written to churches composed chiefly of Gentiles. Had he written to a purely Jewish church, he would most likely have employed the Hebrew name Saul. See Hackett's "Commentary on Acts," 13 : 9, and Farrar's "Life and Work of St. Paul," vol. 1, pp. 355, 356, for a discussion of the apostle's two names.

All the saints. The word 'all,' which occurs again and again (ver. 2, 7, 8, 25; 2 : 17; 4 : 21), springs from the deep affection of the apostle for this particular church, whose beautiful spirit of unity made it possible to include *all* its members without exception in his greeting. The word 'saints' does not imply perfection of character, for it is applied to all Christians alike. It is a term borrowed from the Old Dispensation, and signifies primarily consecration or separation from the world. A man is therefore a 'saint' in the New Testament sense of the word as soon as he is converted and separated from the world. At the same time the word suggests holiness, or perfection of character, as the ultimate goal toward which those who are thus separated from sinners are continually aiming. **In Christ Jesus.**[2] The people of God are separated from the world and devoted to his service only in Christ; that is, by virtue of the regenerating and purifying influences that have flowed from their spiritual union with him. Compare 1 Cor. 1 : 2. **At Philippi.** See "Introduction," pp. 3, 4. It is generally assumed that Philippi was the first place in Europe in which the gospel was preached, because it was the first place in Europe that Paul visited; but the Epistle to the Romans, with its indications of a long-established church there, would imply that long before this the gospel had found a foothold in Rome. **With the bishops and deacons.** In no other epistle does Paul mention the church officers in his salutation, and it is impossible to say with certainty why he does so here, but it may have been the fact of their having been espe-

[1] Δοῦλος means a *bond servant*, or slave of the household, and thus differs from μίσθιος, μισθωτός, *a hired servant*, and from ἀνδράποδον, *a captive slave.*

[2] Christ Jesus is a better supported reading than Jesus Christ. This inverted form of the name is found only in the writings of Paul.

cially active in procuring the gifts which had been forwarded to him. It is not at all unlikely that a letter was sent with those gifts in the name of the brethren, bishops, and deacons, just as the Epistle sent to the churches from the council at Jerusalem was written in the name of "the apostles and the elder brethren." (Acts 15 : 23, Rev. Ver.)

Bishops and presbyters, or elders, are not two different orders of church officers, but are identical, as may be seen by comparing Acts 20 : 17, 28 (overseers, in Greek, bishops), Titus 1 : 5, 7. The same thing appears also from 1 Tim. 3 : 1-13, where the qualifications of a bishop are immediately followed by those of a deacon, with no suggestion of any intermediate order, and from the present passage, where also Paul mentions only bishops and deacons. Now if there had been a third order in the church, why should Paul have omitted any reference to it in First Timothy, where he was enumerating the qualifications of the officers of the church, and in this Epistle, where he refers to the other orders by their respective titles? The absence of any allusion to presbyters or elders, where, if there had been such a distinct order, their name would naturally appear, leads irresistibly to the conclusion that there was no such separate order, and this conclusion is confirmed by the passages above referred to in Acts and Titus, where bishop and elder are used interchangeably for the same office. Even in the First Epistle of Clement to the Corinthians, written about 100 A. D., only two orders are recognized (ch. 42 : 4 compared with 44 : 5), and the same is true of Polycarp's "Epistles to the Philippians," written about twenty years later. (Ch. 5, 6.) Ellicott, while admitting the identity of the two names, bishop and presbyter, or elder, in the New Testament, insists that there are *traces* of the subsequent official distinction between them. See his Notes on 1 Tim. 3 : 1. We fail to find any such traces even as late as Clement and Polycarp. Harnach, in his note on Clement 42 : 4, says: "It is clearer than day that there were only two orders in the clergy at that time, bishops (equivalent to presbyters) and deacons."

With regard to the two names for the same office, bishop and elder, the first, literally overseer, inspector, was the Greek name, and designated the office from the standpoint of its duties; the second was the Jewish name, borrowed from the synagogue, and described the office from the standpoint of its age and dignity. Paul is the only one of the New Testament writers who uses the title of bishop, the others always using the word elder, though Peter calls Christ "the Shepherd and Bishop" of souls. (1 Peter 2 : 25.) The word deacon, as the name of an officer in the church, occurs only here and in 1 Tim. 3 : 8-13. The duties of deacons are nowhere described, although the requisite qualifications for the office are stated in the passage in 1 Tim. 3 : 8-13. While we have no account in the New Testament of the origin of the office of bishop, we have in Acts 6 : 1-6 the probable origin of the deaconship, though the name deacon is not used. The duties of a deacon, as suggested by that narrative, are the oversight and care of the external affairs of the church. Their name, from a verb meaning to serve, implies that they are to be the pastor's helpers or assistants.

Clement, in his first epistle, gives an account of the method of appointing bishops and deacons, which is of great value as indicating the views of the age immediately succeeding the apostolic period. According to his statement, the apostles appointed their first converts as bishops and deacons, and these, in turn, appointed others, with the consent of the whole church. (Ch. 42, 44.) A change is here revealed from those early days, when the people themselves apparently chose their own officers (see Acts 6 : 5), since in Clement's time the officers choose and the people merely confirm, yet it shows that later hierarchical notions had not yet appeared. The officers are still in the church, for the church, and by the church.

The mention of the church officers *after* the body of the church, shows how far Paul's idea of church offices differed from those views about the priesthood which sprung up in later times, and have held sway ever since over so large a portion of Christendom. With him the officers were evidently only a part of the church, not an order separate from and above the laity. Generally in his writings, he makes no distinction between the church officers and the rest of the membership; and even here, where some special, though to us unknown,

2 Grace *be* unto you, and peace, from God our Father and *from* the Lord Jesus Christ.
3 I thank my God upon every remembrance of you.

2 the [1] bishops and deacons: Grace to you and peace from God our Father and the Lord Jesus Christ.
3 I thank my God upon all my remembrance of you,

[1] Or, *overseers*.

reason has led him to mention them specifically by their titles, he nevertheless places them after the body of the church; not, perhaps, with any special purpose, but simply because neither in his mind nor in that of his readers had church offices become associated with any notions of superiority.

2. Grace be unto you, and peace. The greeting is substantially the same as in all the other epistles, except Colossians and First and Second Thessalonians. It is the distinctively Christian form of salutation, blending together and at the same time spiritualizing both the Greek and Hebrew modes. The Greek said "greeting" (χαίρειν), a form which is found also in Acts 15:23; 23:26, and in James 1:1. The Christians seem generally to have shrunk from this form as having a savor of heathenism, and they substituted for it the word 'grace' (χάρις), which, in the Greek, resembles the ordinary word in sound, while it carries the thought infinitely higher, to that disposition of God and Christ from which all our blessings flow. To this word 'grace' they added the word 'peace,' which the Hebrews were accustomed to use whenever they met each other, saying, "Peace to thee," meaning prosperity, every kind of good, but which had become sanctified on the lips of Christ to a still higher significance, when he said: "My peace I give unto you: not as the world giveth (by compliment, in mere words), give I unto you." (John 14:27.) Hence, these two expressions combined denote all spiritual and temporal blessings (peace) from grace, or the undeserved favor of God as their source. "Thus are the forms of common life hallowed by Christian love, and a passing courtesy is transformed into a prayer for heavenly blessings." As we see from the similar salutations of Peter and Jude, where the sentence is completed, the salutation of Paul must be regarded as a prayer, and the verb to be supplied is optative, not imperative. See Winer, p. 585, and 1 Peter 1:2, "be multiplied." The imperative mood would imply an authority to bestow blessings, which, while it is claimed by the Romish Church and others as the peculiar prerogative of the clergy, has no warrant in the New Testament. The benedictions of the apostles are simply prayers, and nothing more; and there is no reason to suppose that one Christian has any more right to use them than another. **From God our Father and from the Lord Jesus Christ.** What a strong, though purely incidental, proof of the divinity of Christ is the combination of his name with that of God the Father in such forms of blessing! What pious Jew, with his lofty conception of the One God, could have combined any inferior name with that sacred name in prayer? The attempt to weaken the force of this form of words by interpreting it to mean "from our Father and (the Father of) the Lord Jesus Christ," is so evidently a makeshift, as to enhance the force of the argument from the usual conjunction of the two names.

3-11. THANKSGIVING FOR THEIR FELLOWSHIP, AND PRAYER FOR THEIR RICHER DEVELOPMENT IN KNOWLEDGE AND DISCERNMENT.—The apostle now proceeds to express his great joy over the favorable condition of the Philippian Church (3, 4), which has continued from his first acquaintance with them until the present moment (5-8); and he prays that this spiritual prosperity may increase yet more and more, until, richly developed in love, knowledge, and spiritual sensibility (9), they shall be prepared, at the great day of judgment, to glorify God by the rich fruitage of righteousness which their lives shall then exhibit (10, 11).

3. I thank my God. For similar expressions, compare Rom. 1:8; 1 Cor. 1:4; Eph. 1:16; Col. 1:3; 1 Thess. 1:2; 2 Thess. 1:3; Philem. 4. He is grateful to God for all the good he sees in the church, the credit for which does not belong to men, but to him who worketh in us "both to will and to do of his good pleasure." (2:13.) What a sense of the nearness of the divine presence in the appropriating words 'my God'! How much he felt bound to give thanks to God in the case of this

4 Always in every prayer of mine for you all making request with joy,
5 For your fellowship in the gospel from the first day until now;

4 always in every supplication of mine on behalf of
5 you all making my supplication with joy, for your fellowship in furtherance of the gospel from the

particular church appears from the words that follow. **Upon[1] every remembrance of you** —a rendering forbidden by the article (Winer, p. 111)—rather, as in the Revised Version, *Upon all my remembrance of you.* Paul declares that his whole remembrance of the Philippian Church fills him with gratitude. As he glances back to the beginning of his acquaintance with them, and reviews his entire remembrance of them up to the present hour, he finds occasion for nothing but thankfulness. See 2 Cor. 8 : 1, seq.

4. Always in every prayer . . . making request with joy. He here states the occasion when this gratitude finds expression—'in every prayer' for them. He never prays for them without giving thanks. His *whole* remembrance causes gratitude, and this finds expression in *every* prayer. The next words describe a feature of his prayers for the Philippian Church, that he mentions in no other epistle. His prayer for them was the outflowing of an entirely joyful heart. How often he prayed for his brethren with grief and tears, but not so for this beautiful church! For them he made the request 'with joy,' for there was nothing in their condition to hinder emotions of gratitude and praise. In these words he strikes the keynote of the Epistle. As Bengel well says, "The whole Epistle is summed up in the words: I rejoice, do ye rejoice." See ver. 18, 25; 2 : 2, 19, 28; 3 : 1; 4 : 1, 4. The word for 'joy' occurs in all thirteen times in the course of this letter.

5. For your fellowship. This was the special element in his remembrance which caused his unalloyed gratitude. It is very difficult to find an exact equivalent in English for the word translated 'fellowship' (κοινωνία), though that word answers better than any other. It means a sharing in anything or participating with any one. Out of this primary meaning grows the occasional signification of gift or contribution. Meyer and Cremer deny that it ever has such a meaning; but see Rom. 15 : 26; 2 Cor. 9 : 13, where any other interpretation is artificial. Some have taken the meaning here to be "gift," but it is impossible that Paul should have expressed such excessive gratitude merely for a material contribution to his support. Those who insist that he must refer to the gifts of the church, because otherwise he would have made no acknowledgment of their kindness at the opening of his letter, and such omission would be a breach of courtesy, apply to the apostle a merely conventional rule, the authority of which he nowhere recognizes. To him the close of the letter seemed the proper place for such acknowledgments, and there he has expressed most fully and beautifully his appreciation of the aid which the Philippian Church sent him. On the other hand, Paul regarded the opening of his Epistle as a place for higher considerations than mere personal matters, and so here he expresses his gratitude for their 'fellowship in the gospel,' that is, their participation in the work of spreading it, their unity of faith and love in carrying it forward. The Revised Version translates the words more accurately than the Common Version, *fellowship in furtherance of the gospel,* for it was not participation in gospel privileges, but fellowship in gospel work of which Paul was thinking. He was thankful that they were so united in gospel service. They had always participated in efforts to extend the gospel, and it was this beautiful spirit of unity in which all distinctions were melted, this common interest for the success of the gospel, which won the apostle's admiration and inspired him with such constant thankfulness to God. "The communion of saints was with them a point of practice, as well as an article of belief." See ver. 27. **From the first day until now.** Even at the very first the preaching of the gospel in Philippi had been followed by marked results (Acts 16 : 13, seq.), but Paul, by the

[1] We have here, and in ver. 5, the same Greek preposition, although in one case it is rendered "upon," and in the other "for." It does not, however, have a different significance in the two cases, as the translation would suggest, but in both designates the basis of the action. His thanksgiving is based in general upon his remembrance of them, and in particular upon one special feature of that remembrance—their fellowship.

6 Being confident of this very thing, that he which hath begun a good work in you will perform *it* until the day of Jesus Christ:

7 Even as it is meet for me to think this of you all, because I have you in my heart; inasmuch as both in

6 first day until now; being confident of this very
thing, that he who began a good work in you will
7 perfect it until the day of Jesus Christ: even as it is
right for me to be thus minded on behalf of you all,
because [1] I have you in my heart, inasmuch as, both

1 Or, *ye have me in your heart.*

words 'until now,' suggests that a similar spirit had characterized the church during its whole history.

6. Being confident of this very thing. Paul now glances into the future, and expresses his hopefulness about that. His remembrance was all joy, his anticipation all hope. **That he** (that is, God), **which hath begun** (Revised Version, *began*) **a good work** (the fellowship spoken of), **will perform it**—more accurately, as in the Revised Version, *will perfect* or *complete it.* The verb in the original signifies to bring to an end, to make complete. **Until the day of Jesus Christ.** The "day of Jesus Christ," or "day of the Lord," is a New Testament phrase for the day of judgment. Compare 1 Cor. 5 : 5; 2 Cor. 1 : 14; 1 Thess. 5 : 2; 2 Peter 3 : 10. The good work begun is not finished at once, but gradually, and reaches its completion only in eternity. Some have inferred from this reference to the day of judgment that Paul supposed it near at hand. Instead of saying that God would carry forward his good work in the hearts of the Philippians until the day of death, which would appear to be the natural terminus—the hour we always have in mind—he says 'until the day of Jesus Christ'; and some able commentators have discovered in this and kindred allusions to that day an expectation of its immediate coming. But such a conclusion is unwarranted. In Paul's thought the day of judgment was paramount; we dwell much on the hour of *death*; he never does. His thoughts overleap all intervening events and spring forward to that longed for day of the Lord's appearing. Even when close upon the hour of his martyrdom he still continues to look forward far beyond the immediate prospect. While he gladly welcomes the release from earthly labors and hardships, he looks beyond the immediate future to "that day," when the crown "laid up" shall be given to him. See 2 Tim. 4 : 6, seq. For further remarks on this subject, see 4 : 5. Calvin has some beautiful and suggestive thoughts upon this distant outlook of the apostle. "Although those who have been freed from the mortal body do no longer contend with the lusts of the flesh, but are, so to express it, beyond the reach of a single dart, yet there will be no absurdity in speaking of them as in the way of advancement, inasmuch as they have not yet reached the point at which they aspire—they do not yet enjoy the felicity and glory which they have hoped for; and, in fine, the day has not yet shone, which is to discover the treasures which lie hid in hope. And in truth, when hope is treated of, our eyes must always be directed forward to the blessed resurrection, as the grand object in view."

7. Even as it is meet (or, *right*[1]) **for me to think this of you**[2] **all.** He is justified in his confidence about their future from the signs of the Christian life which the Philippians have already exhibited. He has it indelibly inscribed upon his heart how in the past they have co-operated with him in all his efforts, and sympathized with him in all his sufferings for the gospel; and as his prayer (ver. 4) embraced them all, so also does his hope—he thinks this of them *all.* **Because I have you in my heart.**[3] They are such Christians that he has taken them into his very heart—they have proved worthy of his deepest love; and hence he looks hopefully toward their future. That he had not taken them into his heart without reason, but in consequence of their Christian character, appears from the following words: **Inasmuch as both**[4] **in my**

[1] The more classical Greek construction would be either the accusative δίκαιον ἐμέ, or the nominative δίκαιος εἰμί.

[2] The preposition ὑπέρ, implies a favorable opinion; περί would be used to express simply the idea "about," without any added suggestion.

[3] The alternative rendering upon the margin of both the Authorized and Revised Versions cannot be justified in view of the context, the singular number 'heart,' and the order of the words. Of course, grammatically it is correct.

[4] The Greek particles τε, καί, show that we have here two related notions of which the second is the more important. The first notion is contained in the words,

my bonds, and in the defence and confirmation of the gospel, ye all are partakers of my grace.
8 For God is my record, how greatly I long after you all in the bowels of Jesus Christ.

in my bonds and in the defence and confirmation of the gospel, ye all are partakers with me of grace.
8 For God is my witness, how I long after you all in

bonds, and in the defence and confirmation of the gospel, ye all are partakers of my grace. Some connect these words differently both with each other and with the preceding words; thus, Because I have you in my heart, both in my bonds, and in the defence and confirmation of the gospel, ye all being partakers with me of grace. According to this arrangement we have here expressed the *greatness* of the apostle's love. He thinks of them even amid the trials of his imprisonment, and his arduous labors in behalf of the gospel. None of these things could divert his thoughts from them, or weaken the strength of his attachment to them. This view of the passage has the sanction of many eminent expositors, Dr. Hackett among the number. But the other arrangement of the words, which is that of both the Common and the Revised Versions, is to be preferred. According to that, Paul expresses here the *reason* of his great love for the Philippians. He has them in his heart, because they have always been in such close and tender sympathy with him in all his labors and sufferings. They had endeavored to alleviate his sufferings while a prisoner, and to sustain and encourage his efforts in defending and advancing the cause of Christ. How, then, could such a great-hearted man as Paul help taking them into his very heart after such manifestations of love, or entertain other than the most hopeful views of their future after such convincing evidences of Christian fellowship? The 'defence and confirmation' describes the twofold method of prosecuting the work of the gospel, by answering objections and removing obstacles and prejudices—the defence: and by establishing and confirming the faith of believers, so that they may become "grounded and settled"—the confirmation. We have an example of the defence of the gospel in Acts 28 : 17-24, and a notable illustration of its confirmation in Paul's letters to the various churches. In all this experience the Philippians have been partakers with the apostle in the grace of God, for Paul regarded it as a grace to be permitted to preach the gospel (see Eph. 3 : 8), and to suffer for it. See ver. 29, where the words "it is given" hint in the original at the divine favor in the privilege. This special favor of God the Philippians had shared by participating so zealously in the apostle's work and trials. They had ministered to him in bonds, and sustained his spirit in his vast labors, and it was entirely in harmony with Paul's noble nature, to dignify their sympathy by suggesting that it was all a mark of the divine favor. Thus their work was elevated to a lofty plain, and they were encouraged to enter with alacrity upon future tasks. The word 'partakers' by its similarity of sound and meaning in the original with the word translated 'fellowship' (ver. 5), brings again vividly before the mind that beautiful spirit of fraternity which characterized the church; their fellowship with each other was also a fellowship with the apostle.

8. For God is my record (or, *witness*). For similar forms of attestation, see Rom. 1 : 9; 2 Cor. 1 : 23; 1 Thess. 2 : 5, 10. **How greatly I long after you all in the bowels of Jesus Christ.** These words confirm his previous statement, that he has them in his heart, by a striking metaphor—I not only have you in my heart, but that heart is the very heart of Christ himself, who abides within me (Gal. 2 : 20), and whose heart beats in my bosom. The word 'bowels' is very common with Paul, and is borrowed from the Hebrew. It has not a pleasant sound in English, and the Revised Version has put "tender mercies" in its place, but this destroys the apostle's image entirely, and gives us prose instead of poetry. The word *heart* would be a better rendering, although not quite so accurate as 'bowels,' for it would harmonize better with our modes of speech. We express by this word that idea of sympathy and tender affection which the Hebrew conveyed by the word bowels. Generally Paul says "in Christ," simply; but he doubtless chose this special word because he

'in my bonds,' which describe the apostle's condition, the second in the combined expression 'the defence and confirmation of the gospel,' which describes his employment. The single article before the two words 'defence and confirmation,' combine them into a single conception.

9 And this I pray, that your love may abound yet
more and more in knowledge and *in* all judgment;
10 That ye may approve things that are excellent;
that ye may be sincere and without offence till the day
of Christ;

9 the tender mercies of Christ Jesus. And this I pray,
that your love may abound yet more and more in
10 knowledge and all discernment; so that ye may [1] approve the things that are excellent; that ye may be
sincere and void of offence unto the day of Christ;

[1] *Or, prove the things that differ.*

wished to give peculiar warmth and tenderness to his language.

9. And this I pray. Having stated the cause of the thankfulness expressed in ver. 3, he now gives the purport of the prayer alluded to in ver. 4. It is Paul's way in writing to the churches, first of all, to praise their characteristic excellencies, and then to suggest their characteristic defects. So here he begins by extolling the fellowship of the church, and then delicately hints at their need of greater knowledge and judgment by telling them that the increase of their love in these particulars forms the subject of his constant prayer. **Your love.** This word denotes that inward state of the soul already described as 'fellowship.' Love is not exactly identical with fellowship, but rather its root and support, so that while recalling the latter word it suggests at the same time the source of that beautiful fraternity. The Greek word here used (ἀγάπη), though the usual one in the New Testament, is not found in profane writers, and was apparently coined by the Alexandrian translators of the Old Testament. The ordinary Greek terms for love seem to have been too weak to express the Hebrew conception, for while the Greek language had the strongest expressions of hatred and enmity, it had no words descriptive of love in its divine greatness. **May abound[1] yet more and more in knowledge and in all judgment.** Paul does not pray for a mere increase of their love, for this was already a distinguishing characteristic of the church, but for a development of love in the direction of sound knowledge and right moral perceptions. Their love needed to become more intelligent and discriminating; without knowledge and judgment, love is apt to be misplaced and to become the sport of every impulse. The apostle desires that they shall be able to distinguish the true from the false, and shall not love indiscriminately. "Love without knowledge is blind; knowledge without love is cold." We have probably a hint here of the characteristic defect in the religious life of the Philippian Church—the more thoughtful side was still undeveloped—while the Corinthian Church, on the other hand, appears pre-eminently intellectual, but lacking in humility and unity. See 1 Cor. 1: 4-10. The word translated knowledge in the text denotes a full and more complete knowledge. See 1 Cor. 13: 12, where the simple and the compound words appear in a most instructive contrast. The word 'judgment' (Common Version), 'discernment' (Revised Version), signifies discrimination, moral tact (De Wette)—that inward perception which guides right in morals as by a kind of instinct. "The soul also hath her senses as well as the body." (Trapp.) The Greek word occurs only here in the New Testament, though a related word appears in Heb. 5: 14, signifying organs of moral sense. Compare Jer. 4: 9.

10. This verse is rendered in two ways: **That ye may approve things that are excellent** (Common Version; Revised Version), or, **That ye may try** (prove) **the things that differ** (margins of both versions). The difference between these two renderings is not important, for both processes must have a place. If we distinguish things that differ, it is for the sake of approving what is excellent, and *vice versa*, if we approve things that are excellent, it must be in consequence of having distinguished between things that differ. Meyer prefers the first rendering, because it describes a higher moral act, but the second harmonizes better with the word 'judgment,' which suggests a sifting process. In this process, as Bengel well says, we are not merely to distinguish the good from the bad, but the best among the good, whose excellence none but the more advanced perceive. Paul has here given us a true description of Christian wisdom, love growing continually richer in knowledge and moral discernment. **That ye may be sincere and without offence** describes the result of the moral discipline obtained by exercising the spiritual faculties in distinguishing things that differ. The word

[1] The present tense of the verb denotes continuous growth.

11 Being filled with the fruits of righteousness, which are by Jesus Christ, unto the glory and praise of God.
12 But I would ye should understand, brethren, that the things *which happened* unto me have fallen out rather unto the furtherance of the gospel;

11 being filled with the [1] fruits of righteousness, which are through Jesus Christ, unto the glory and praise of God.
12 Now I would have you know, brethren, that the things *which happened* unto me have fallen out rather

1 Gr. *fruit.*

'sincere' means, literally, "tested by the sunlight." Hence, it is a very picturesque and strong description of Christian purity. 'Without offence'—that is, causing no one to stumble, leading no one to sin. Compare 1 Cor. 10:32. In these two expressions, 'pure' and 'without offence,' we have a positive and negative description of blamelessness. The first word also refers more directly to their relations with God; the second to their relations with men. **Till** (or, *unto*) **the day of Christ** describes the all-important time when this character shall be revealed, and therefore a day ever to be kept in mind.

11. Being filled with the fruits of righteousness. Paul is not satisfied with purity and harmlessness, but desires a fullness of Christian graces. 'The fruits of righteousness' are true and right actions, moral and spiritual obedience. 'Righteousness' is not here the righteousness of faith—that is, that righteousness which faith appropriates—but rectitude of conduct, that righteousness which faith reflects, as the dewdrop reflects the sun. **Which are by Jesus Christ,** who is the only source of such good actions. Christ must abide in us before we can bear fruits of righteousness. See John 15:4. **Unto the glory and praise of God,** the end and aim of all fruit bearing. 'Glory' denotes the divine majesty, and 'praise' the acknowledgment of that divine majesty among men. Good works, or 'fruits of righteousness,' display the divine glory, because all goodness in man has its origin in God, and hence men are led to praise God whenever they behold this particular manifestation of his glory. See Matt. 5:16. In Eph. 1:6 we have a slightly different expression for the idea in the text: "to the praise of the glory of his grace."

In this beautiful outpouring of the apostle's heart, we obtain one of the clearest glimpses into his loving and tender nature that any of his writings afford. Other epistles reveal more fully his wonderful knowledge, his logical power, his profound thought, his bold and lofty spirit, but none reveals to us so clearly as this the depths of his heart. Here the stream of loving, tender words flows on, unflecked and unruffled, and in it we see, as in a mirror, the perfect lineaments of a most noble nature.

12-26. The Apostle's Condition at Rome and his State of Feeling.—He informs them of the effect of his imprisonment upon the cause of Christ (12-14), magnanimously declares, in view of the insincerity of some of the preachers of the gospel, that he takes account of nothing else but the fact, that Christ is preached (15-18), and calmly revolves the question whether life or death is to be the issue of his present condition (19-26).

12. But I would ye should understand—or, *Now I would have you know, brethren.* (Revised Version). The suggestion of Wiesinger, that the church may have addressed him some questions concerning the effect of his imprisonment upon the cause of Christ, and that this accounts for the suddenness of the transition, seems highly probable. Naturally, the church, on hearing the circumstances of his visit to Rome, would be fearful lest the fact of his being a prisoner, in chains, might prove detrimental to the gospel; and what so likely as that in their solicitude they should question him about it? At any rate, whether informed of their anxiety or only surmising it, the apostle hastens to remove it by declaring that, strange as it may appear, all had resulted in good. **That the things which happened unto me**[1]—the imprisonment and attendant circumstances. **Have fallen out rather unto the furtherance of the gospel,** than the opposite, as might have been feared. How characteristic is all this of Paul! Nowhere does he dwell on the hardships of his lot, but ever sets before the reader its hopeful features. He had intended to visit Rome, when his work in

[1] In late writers, the preposition κατά, with a personal pronoun, becomes almost equivalent to the possessive, so that τὰ κατ' ἐμέ is equivalent to τὰ ἐμά, literally, my affairs.

13 So that my bonds in Christ are manifest in all the palace, and in all other *places*;

13 unto the progress of the gospel; so that my bonds became manifest in Christ [1] throughout the whole

[1] Gr. *in the whole Prætorium.*

Asia and Greece should be finished, but he had not expected to be carried there a prisoner. Yet this very circumstance was undoubtedly a help to his work; his acquaintance with the soldiers obtained for him an opening at Rome even in Cæsar's household (4:22), which he would probably otherwise have sought in vain. Of course, this was due to God's overruling providence, which makes even the wrath of man to praise him. (Ps. 76:10.) Paul might say to his enemies, as Joseph said to his brethren: "Ye thought evil against me; but God meant it unto good." (Gen. 50:20.)

13. So that my bonds in Christ are manifest—better, *have become manifest in Christ.* One way in which his imprisonment helped to further the gospel was by making his bonds manifest in Christ to the soldiers who guarded him, and through them to others. The words 'in Christ' should be connected with 'manifest,' not, as in the Common Version, with 'my bonds.' The simple manifesting of his bonds, or making him known as a prisoner, would not have helped the gospel; but the manifesting of them in Christ—that is, revealing them as borne in Christ's service and for his sake—did benefit the gospel. The whole emphasis of the sentence should be laid upon the words 'manifest in Christ'; for this was the feature of his imprisonment that was of importance. Instead of being regarded as a common criminal who had committed some great and disgraceful crime, as would naturally have been the case, he was soon known as a prisoner for the sake of his religion; he was recognized as "a prisoner of the Lord" (Eph. 4:1), suffering "as a Christian" (1 Peter 4:16). Compare Acts 28:20; Eph. 6:20. Thus his bonds served to preach Christ; for they proclaimed to all beholders how much he valued the gospel, since he was willing to be bound for its sake. **In all the palace.** The word translated 'palace' means, primarily, a general's tent or headquarters. It was then applied to the camp or barracks of the prætorian guard, or emperor's body guard, at Rome, which was built on the east of the city, just outside of the Viminal gate, and also to the residences of governors in the provinces (Matt. 27:27, et al.), and even to the palaces of kings (Juvenal 10:161); but there is no instance of its application to the imperial residence at Rome, which is called "Cæsar's house" in 4:22, nor is it likely that it would be so applied, as it had become the technical name for the governors' residences in the provinces. The imperial residence on the Palatine hill seems to have included a portion of the barracks of the prætorian guard, and the word may have been applied to *that portion* of the residence, but never to the palace as a whole. Lightfoot translates "prætorian guard," and so also does the Revised Version; but Dr. Hackett well says that "with that direct personal sense, we might have expected the dative without 'in' (ἐν), as in the other clause (compare Acts 4:16; 7:13; 1 Tim. 5:15), whereas, with the local sense as the direct one, and the personal as indirect, the change of construction becomes perfectly natural." (Lange's "Commentary," p. 20.) In Acts 23:35 we find the word used of the place of Paul's imprisonment at Cesarea; and those who believe the Epistle to have been written during Paul's stay there, base their argument almost wholly on this correspondence in the words designating his place of imprisonment. See "Introduction," p. 5. In Acts 28:16 we learn that Paul dwelt in his own hired house; but even if this were outside of the barracks, he must still have been guarded constantly by an attendant soldier, who would have the opportunity of hearing him preach and of learning both the facts of his personal history and of the gospel story; and as the soldiers relieved each other in turn, a large number would come gradually to know the true state of the case—the real reasons for the apostle's imprisonment—and would naturally spread such interesting facts throughout a still wider circle, until they became known through the whole prætorian camp. **And in all other places**—or, as in Revised Version, *And to all the rest* (others beside the prætorian guard). He does not mean that all the rest of the people of Rome heard of the true cause of his imprisonment, but declares, in a popular and hyperbolical way, that a great many did.

14 And many of the brethren in the Lord, waxing confident by my bonds, are much more bold to speak the word without fear.
15 Some indeed preach Christ even of envy and strife; and some also of good will:

14 prætorian guard, and to all the rest; and that most
of the brethren in the Lord, [1] being confident through
my bonds, are more abundantly bold to speak the
15 word of God without fear. Some indeed preach
Christ even of envy and strife; and some also of good

[1] Gr. *trusting in my bonds.*

Compare Matt. 3:5. While all the Roman citizens did not learn the facts of the case, those who did learn them were very likely to get a true statement of the cause of his confinement, and discovered that he was no common criminal.

14. And many of the brethren in the Lord, waxing confident by my bonds. A better translation would be: *And most of the brethren being confident in the Lord through my bonds.* Another effect of his imprisonment was to encourage the brethren, not all of them, but the majority. There was still a small minority who manifested a cowardly and unworthy spirit, but the greater part, seeing the spirit in which Paul endured his imprisonment for Christ's sake, became more courageous themselves. The inspiring example of Paul, his hopefulness and cheerfulness. even in bonds, encouraged these brethren to lay hold with firmer faith upon the promises of God. The apostle's bonds were a tangible evidence of his faith in the gospel, and so they wonderfully affected the brethren, for very often the eye of the body influences the eye of the soul. The words 'in the Lord' should be connected with 'being confident,' and not, as in the Common and Revised Versions, with 'brethren.' Their confidence was in God, otherwise Paul's bonds would have produced dismay instead of courage. 'In the Lord' describes the cause, and 'through my bonds' the occasion of their confidence. **Are much more bold** than if he were not a prisoner. **To speak the word without fear.** The implication is that they had already ventured to speak before this, but with some degree of fear. "Had he when in bonds taken it hardly, and held his peace, it were probable that they would be affected in like manner. But as he spoke more boldly when in bonds, he gave them more confidence than if he had not been bound." (Chrysostom.) The accumulation of emphatic phrases, 'being confident,' 'much more bold,' 'without fear,' springs from the apostle's overflowing heart, like the emphatic repetition, 'all,' 'always,' 'every,' in ver. 3, 4, and the accumulated expression in ver. 9, 10.

15. Some indeed preach Christ even of envy and strife. Not all the brethren have been made confident in the Lord by the apostle's bonds Some are taking occasion from his imprisonment to show a very different spirit. The preachers here described cannot be a portion of those already mentioned in ver. 14, for those brethren are portrayed in entirely different colors from these; but we have here a description of that minority already hinted at in the words 'most of the brethren.' These preach from 'envy and strife,' from wrong motives, from envy of Paul's influence and success, and for the sake of exciting strife in the church. The very main spring of their activity is therefore a desire to injure Paul and to destroy his influence. "So it is possible to do a good work from a motive which is not good." (Chrysostom.) Who these opposers were cannot be determined, but the general view, that they were the Judaizing party, seems opposed to the fact that Paul rejoiced over their efforts, because thereby Christ was preached. The difficulty with these brethren seems to lie in their motives rather than their doctrine. Paul's words in ver. 18 certainly imply this, for he says that Christ is preached by both parties, but by the one in pretence, by the other in truth; that is, the one party was honest, the other dishonest; but if they had been Judaizers the difference would have been of another kind. Such indications as this—and they are by no means infrequent—show that the popular notion of the apostolic churches, as far superior to those of any subsequent period, is, to say the least, very doubtful. **And some also of good will.** These are the same as those mentioned in ver. 14, but introduced here again under a different point of view, and in contrast with those just described. These preach from 'good will,' the opposite of 'envy and strife.' Their motive was a personal one also, but how noble and pure, good will toward one who was the appointed de-

16 The one preach Christ of contention, not sincerely, supposing to add affliction to my bonds:
17 But the other of love, knowing that I am set for the defence of the gospel.

16 will: [1] the one *do it* of love, knowing that I am set
17 for the defence of the gospel: [2] but the other proclaim Christ of faction, not sincerely, thinking to

[1] Or, *they that are moved by love do it*......[2] Or, *but they that are factious proclaim Christ.*

fender of the gospel, whose work they regarded as a holy work, which it was their duty to help forward, especially now that by his imprisonment he himself was hindered to a great extent from carrying out his mission. The word 'good will' is generally used of the divine good pleasure, as in 2 : 13, but it is also used of man's good will in Rom. 10 : 1.

16, 17. The Received Text reverses the true order of these verses, probably for the sake of symmetry in the course of thought. According to the correct arrangement, observed in the Revised Version, the subject last mentioned in the preceding verse is discussed first in this. Such irregularities are not uncommon in other writers. The rhetorical name for such an arrangement of words or clauses is a chiasmus, or chiasma. The order should be as follows: **The one** [*do it*] **of love;** better, *the one of love do it*, that is, preach Christ, as suggested in ver. 15. Compare rendering on the margin of Revised Version. In the Common and the Revised Versions the words 'of love' are connected with the predicate: 'The one do it of love'; but in this case we have repeated again the motive of their preaching, which has once been given already; so that it is better to take the words as belonging to the subject, as in the kindred expressions, "they which are of faith" (Gal. 3 : 7), "every one that is of the truth" (John 18 : 37), etc., in which case they characterize their prevailing spirit. They are 'of love,' the love party; love is their nature; from love they derive their very life; it is the fountain whence all their activity flows. **Knowing that I am set for the defence of the gospel** unfolds more fully the nature of their motive, mentioned in ver. 15. Their 'good will' was not directed merely toward his person, but included his work, and was in fact chiefly based upon that. This 'good will' was but another phase of their general spirit of love, which, being of God (1 John 4 : 7), naturally embraced the person of one so devoted to God's work. On the verb 'set,' compare Luke 2 : 34; 1 Thess. 3 : 3; also 1 Cor. 9 : 16, "Necessity is laid upon me." **But the other preach Christ of contention**—better, *Of contentiousness proclaim Christ.* Compare margin of Revised Version. See the same Greek phrase in Rom. 2 : 8. These are the envious party, whose motives have already been described in ver. 15. The word translated 'contentiousness' signifies intrigue or party spirit, and includes both the envy and strife of ver. 15. In Gal. 5 : 20 Paul mentions this among the works of the flesh. These contentious ones, like the love party, 'proclaim Christ,' which words might have been omitted, as in the preceding verse, but are added to bring out the baseness of their motives: they proclaim Christ, attempt such holy work—not purely, etc. The Greek verb here used does not differ materially from that in the preceding verse. Literally, the former signifies to announce, as a messenger, the latter to proclaim, as a herald; but both are used indiscriminately of preaching. Although this party preach Christ, it is not with a pure and honest purpose. The apostle does not strictly impute hypocrisy to them, as the words 'not sincerely' of the Common Version and the Revised Version would suggest, but rather a spirit of narrow-minded partisanship and personal hostility. Chrysostom probably expresses the truth when he represents them as jealous of the apostle. **Supposing to add affliction to my bonds.** "His bonds were already an affliction; they were adding affliction to the afflicted." (Bengel.) The word 'supposing' (οἰόμενοι), used by Paul nowhere else, is aptly chosen to hint that their purpose was not realized, and forms a suggestive contrast with the word 'knowing' (εἰδότες) of the previous verse.[1] Those have knowledge, these mere supposition. They supposed that their animosity and personal enmity would add or raise up (Revised Version founded upon a better reading) affliction; that is, make his imprisonment more distressing by causing his spirit to chafe against the chains that held him, as he beheld his opponents having such

[1] Compare Plato's "Apology," 41 D, where Socrates uses the words οἰόμενοι βλάπτειν with the same idea of the futility of the effort.

18 What then? notwithstanding, every way, whether
in pretence, or in truth, Christ is preached; and I therein do rejoice, yea, and will rejoice.
19 For I know that this shall turn to my salvation
through your prayer, and the supply of the Spirit of
Jesus Christ,

18 raise up affliction for me in my bonds. What then?
only that in every way, whether in pretence or in
truth, Christ is proclaimed; and therein I rejoice,
19 yea, and will rejoice. For I know that this shall
turn to my salvation, through your supplication and

---

a free field for their pernicious undertaking. In this, however, they were mistaken, as the sequel shows.

18. What then? What then is the state of the case so far as I am concerned? The question implies that he is in no despondent state of mind about it. **Notwithstanding** (better, as in Revised Version, '*Only that*,' only this is the case) 'that in every way'—that is, of preaching—more exactly defined by what follows—'whether in pretence, or in truth, Christ is preached.' The party of contentiousness would, of course, claim to be preaching Christ from love, but as this was not their motive, they were really making a pretence; the professed motive was not the real motive. Compare Mark 12 : 40; Luke 20 : 47. **And I therein,** that is, in the fact that Christ is preached, no matter how, **do rejoice.** These false brethren do not succeed in disturbing the mind of the Great Apostle, which is generous enough to rejoice in their efforts, even though they are prompted by personal hostility to himself. He sees the "soul of goodness in things evil." He sees that there is truth even in such preaching—Christ is presented as the hope of sinners, the knowledge of Christ is diffused more widely, and this is enough to give him joy. Whatever imperfections there may have been in the substance or spirit of their teaching, even an imperfect Christianity was better than the gross heathenism that prevailed everywhere. What a glorious glimpse we have here into the apostle's heart. Never was a more generous and noble sentiment about one's personal enemies uttered than this of Paul's. Self is forgotten, and the interests of truth are all in all. Compare Mark 9 : 40: "Jesus said, Forbid him not, he that is not against us is on our part." In opposition to the misuse of this passage, Calvin well says: "But though Paul rejoiced in the increase of the gospel, he would never have ordained such ministers, had the matter been in his hands." Those who suppose these opponents to be Judaizers, find it difficult to account for the fact that Paul rejoices in their success. His feelings are very different toward those mentioned in 3 : 2, seq., whom some suppose to be identical with those here referred to. The view that these teachers must have been Judaizers seems to have sprung from the feeling, that it was impossible for Christian teachers to have acted in opposition to Paul, but Wiesinger well answers this: "It will require to be proved that there could not be then, as well as now, men who sought their own honor in the preaching of the gospel, and whose hearts were far from the truth which their lips uttered." **Yea, and will** (or, *shall*) **rejoice.** He not only rejoices now, but shall in future. The translations of both the Common and Revised Versions produce an impression that the original does not warrant, that the apostle resolutely combats all tendency to despondency, and says, "I *will* rejoice," as if he were to say, "I am determined to see only the bright side." The original is, however, simple future without any idea of resolve. Besides, it should be connected more closely with what follows, rather than with the preceding words.

19. For I know confirms these statements about his joy, by the assurance that only good can come out of this opposition. Compare Rom. 8 : 28. It gives the reason for both his present and his future rejoicing. His enemies cannot now or at any future time deprive him of his joy. **That this shall turn to my salvation**—that is, this state of affairs in which Christ is preached both from pure and impure motives. 'This' refers to the same thing as 'therein.' (Ver. 18.) There he declares this twofold preaching to be an occasion of joy; here he asserts that it shall procure for him 'salvation,' instead of affliction, as his enemies purposed. (Ver. 16.) The word 'salvation' cannot mean here eternal life, which comes to us purely through the work of Christ; nor can it mean the saving of others, for the personal pronoun "my" refers the matter entirely to the apostle himself. The word must be understood in its most general sense, as well-being, without any attempt to define it more precisely, for it is only as he proceeds that the apostle announces how far and in what way he

20 According to my earnest expectation and *my* hope, that in nothing I shall be ashamed, but *that* with all boldness, as always, *so* now also Christ shall be magnified in my body, whether *it be* by life, or by death.

20 the supply of the Spirit of Jesus Christ, according to my earnest expectation and hope, that in nothing shall I be put to shame, but *that* with all boldness, as always, *so* now also Christ shall be magnified in my body, whether by life, or by death.

expects good results out of this state of affairs. Compare Job 13 : 6, where the Greek of the Septuagint is exactly the same as the words here, and the word 'salvation' has the same general sense. **Through your prayer and the supply of the Spirit of Jesus Christ.** The envy and strife would turn out to his well being by inducing the Philippians to pray for him more fervently, and thus securing for him a larger supply of the Holy Spirit, a greater portion of divine grace. A more accurate translation would be: *Through your prayer and supply of the spirit of Jesus Christ.* We almost shrink from such a bold expression, and yet it is the apostle's language accurately interpreted. He conceived of the Philippians as actually supplying him with the Spirit—of course by means of their prayers, for the two words, prayer and supply, are bound closely together in the Greek by a single article.[1] The prayers of the Philippians are the efficient agency in securing the blessing he looks for. Compare James 5 : 16. What an evidence of the high value which the apostle placed upon intercessory prayer. "He who depends for help on the prayers of saints, relies on the promise of God." (Calvin.) The Greek word for 'supply' perhaps retains something of its primitive meaning "defraying the expenses of a chorus," in the suggestion of the amplitude of the gift and the liberality of the giver. 'The Spirit of Jesus Christ' is the Holy Spirit, so designated here, because Jesus has and bestows the Spirit. (John 15 : 26; Rom. 8 : 9; Gal. 4 : 6; 2 Cor. 3 ; 17; 1 Peter 1 : 11.) The exaltation of the Redeemer secured him the prerogative of bestowing the Spirit upon his followers. (John 16 : 7; Acts 2 : 33.)

20. According to my earnest expectation and my hope. The assurance, that his spiritual welfare will be the result, is in harmony with his 'expectation and hope,' which are unfolded in the following words. The Greek word for 'expectation' found only here and Rom. 8 : 19, signifies patient, persistent looking for, till the fulfillment is realized; literally, it means to look away toward anything, with the head bent forward, so that the use of this word presented a very picturesque suggestion to the readers of the Epistle. **That in nothing,** in no respect, neuter; not masculine, in no person. **Shall I be ashamed.** His long expected mission to the great metropolis seems to have been thwarted by bonds, and likely to be cut short by death, but he trusts it will not prove a failure and cast shame upon him. Though a fettered prisoner, deserted and traduced by those who ought to have been his friends, and without any favor among those in power, he is full of hope and courage. He believes that now, as heretofore, he shall suffer no disgrace, but whatever the result of his imprisonment may be, whether life or death, Christ shall be magnified in him, and he can ask no greater glory for himself than that. Some give to the verb the meaning of failing in duties, so that the apostle declares that he will not fail in any respect to perform his full duty, but Meyer well says, that it is not the behavior, but the fate of the apostle that is under discussion. Compare Prov. 13 : 5; 1 John 2 : 28. **But** has here its full adversative force, but, on the contrary. **That with all boldness.** 'All' complete, entire. 'Boldness'; that is, of speech, the opposite of the state of one put to shame, who is naturally silent. See 1 John 2 : 28, where boldness and shame are contrasted as here. **As always, so now also Christ shall be magnified.** Instead of being put to shame, and disgraced in any way, he expects now, as always heretofore, to be highly honored, for he can receive no greater honor than to be made the instrument of glorifying his Lord. **In my body**—the theatre on which Christ will display his glory. **Whether by life or by death.** Two alternatives suggested by the last words 'in my body.' Whichever of the two alternatives may come to pass, whether his life be preserved, or destroyed, Christ will be honored,—

[1] The article and pronoun in the Greek belong to both nouns, combining them into a single expression, and justifying the translation and interpretation given above. See Buttmann's "Grammar of the New Testament Greek," p. 100.

21 For to me to live *is* Christ, and to die *is* gain.
22 But if I live in the flesh, this *is* the fruit of my labour: yet what I shall choose I wot not.

21 For to me to live is Christ, and to die is gain. [1]But
22 if to live in the flesh—*if* [2]this shall bring fruit from my work, then [3]what I shall choose I know not.

1 Or, *But if to live in the flesh be my lot, this is the fruit of my work: and what I shall choose I know not*......2 Gr. *this is for me fruit of work*......3 Or, *what shall I choose?*

if life is continued, by his apostolic labors, or if he meet a martyr's fate, by his steadfast courage in death. In the latter case, conscious of his great gain, he will die with such unfaltering courage and holy joy, as to reflect honor on his Lord, by revealing his sustaining power in such an hour, so that whatever the result may be, life or death, his boldness and Christ's glory will be made manifest. "He removes ignominy from himself; he ascribes the boldness to himself, the glory to Christ." (Bengel.) The change from the first person in 'I shall be ashamed' to the third person in 'Christ shall be magnified,' shows the apostle's delicate sensitiveness. He shrinks from saying "I shall magnify Christ." Compare similar thoughts in 1 Cor. 6 : 20; 2 Cor. 4 : 10. We have now the full development of that word 'salvation.' (Ver. 19.) This opposition of his enemies will lead only to his good by calling forth earnest prayers in his behalf, which will secure him a larger supply of divine grace, and fulfill his hope of always being made the instrument of Christ's glory, both in life and death.

21. This verse confirms the last words of ver. 20, 'whether by life, or by death.' **To me** is placed first with emphasis; however it may be with others, this is the case *with me.* Life is but another name for Christ; his whole being and activities are his Lord's. "If he traveled, it was on Christ's errand; if he suffered, it was in Christ's service; when he spoke, his theme was Christ; and when he wrote, Christ filled his letters." These words do not mean exactly the same as the "Christ liveth in me" of Gal. 2 : 20. There Christ appears as the source of life, here as the aim and object of life. The truth expressed in Galatians stands related to this as cause to effect. Because Christ lives in him, he could also say, **to me[1] to live is Christ**—that is, *I live for Christ.* **To die is gain,** because he will thereby be brought into a still nearer and more blessed union with his Lord. Paul might with truth have said, to live is Christ, and to die is Christ also, for immediately afterward he describes death as being with Christ, but realizing that death brings a far higher and more perfect union between the believer and his Lord, which such a parallelism would not suggest, he varies the phrase, and says, death is gain, thereby indicating the superiority of death over life from the standpoint of a believer's happiness. An ancient orator said that when life is burdensome death is a gain, and Socrates, in the famous "Apology," declares, that if death should only prove to be a dreamless sleep, it would be a wonderful gain; but how far such utterances fall below this inspired declaration of the apostle! It was not impatience with life that transfigured and glorified death in his eyes. He was not simply weary of life's burdens and anxious to lay them down, he did not welcome death as a cessation of all thought and feeling, but he looked on death as but the door to a new and more glorious existence. Compare 2 Cor. 5 : 1, seq.

22. As this verse is very perplexing, and many different interpretations of it have been given, it may help us to an understanding of its meaning, if we keep the following points in mind. **But** serves to introduce a new consideration. He checks the flow of raptured thought to suggest a consideration that makes him hesitate in his choice between life and death. **If I live in the flesh.** The word 'if' does not in the Greek, as in the English, suggest a kind of uncertainty, as if he were questioning in his own mind whether it were so or not, but it comes nearer to our word "since"; it does not put a problematical case, but a real case forward; what follows is the real state of the case. Compare the same use of the word in Rom. 5 : 17; 6 : 5. Hence he says, 'since living in the flesh is fruit of my work.' But in order to call attention emphatically to that idea of earthly life in contradistinction to the painful death of which he had just spoken so glowingly, he stops and repeats his thought: 'since living in the flesh—since this is for me

[1] Of the two infinitives the first is present, and denotes the state of living; the second is aorist and marks the moment of transition to another world.

23 For I am in a strait betwixt two, having a desire to depart, and to be with Christ; which is far better:

23 But I am in a strait betwixt the two, having the desire to depart and be with Christ; for it is very far

fruit of my work.' The words 'in the flesh' are added to the words 'to live,' because he wishes to fix the attention upon the fact that it is the earthly life he is speaking of. 'Fruit of my work' means fruit that comes from work. For this meaning of 'fruit,' see Rom. 1 : 13. For 'work' as designating the preaching of the gospel, see Acts 13 : 2; 1 Thess. 5 : 13. The meaning then so far is, since earthly life produces fruit from my apostolic labors, brings souls into the kingdom of the Lord. **Yet**—or, *then.* 'Then' introduces the apodosis, or conclusion; if all this be true, if life, and life only, subserves my apostolic work, 'then' comes the difficulty of choice, and **what I shall choose I wot not,** or, *I cannot tell.* 'What'—that is, *which of the two,* death or life. 'Choose,' the Greek verb, has the proper force of the middle voice, *choose for myself.* The words translated 'I wot not' Meyer declares to mean 'I do not make known,' and justifies this interpretation by the fact that everywhere in the New Testament this verb means to make known, to declare, never simply to know. The Revised Version has placed this translation upon the margin. The meaning of the entire verse is then: since earthly life and that alone is the sphere of work, with its blessed fruitage of converted souls, I am so uncertain what to chose, that I refrain from any decision.

Paul was aware that for himself death was gain, and so far as his personal interests were concerned he had no difficulty in choosing, but the blessed results of living cause hesitation and embarrassment. With the two alternatives before him, and in the state of divided feeling they produce, he is so perplexed that he refrains from any choice, not knowing what is best, and preferring to leave it all to the divine disposal. He does not make known even to himself, as Bengel suggests, what he would prefer. But the claims of his work, the needs of the church, gradually assert themselves and take possession of his mind. In such fruit as he can gather by living, there is a gain that outweighs any mere personal considerations; and this fact soon leads him to declare his conviction that he will remain in the body, because his services are so much needed. (Ver. 25.) He is willing to resign the gain for the sake of the fruit. "How hath he both cast out the desire of the present life, and yet thrown no reproach upon it." (Chrysostom.)

23. In this and the next verse, Paul explains more fully the state of uncertainty which he has just described in the words 'what I shall choose,' etc The verb translated 'I am in a strait' signifies to be hemmed in or confined; as in Luke 8 : 45, and is generally associated with the notion of distress, as in Luke 19 : 43; especially in connection with disease, as in Matt. 4 : 24; Luke 4 : 38; Acts 28 : 8. Our Lord uses it also of his own mental distress in Luke 12 : 50. The word serves to express forcibly the intensity of the struggle in Paul's mind.[1] The word **two** refers back to the two alternatives, life and death. Paul's mind is so hemmed in between these two alternatives that he does not know which way to move. Most men would have no trouble in making a quick choice between them. But not so Paul; and, in fact, if he were to choose for his own pleasure, it would be to depart out of this world, that which most men dread more than all the ills of life. **Having a desire to depart**—or, rather, *a desire toward departure.* He does not exactly say, 'having a desire to depart,'[2] as in the Common Version, but declares that his desire is *in that direction.* The verb is a nautical expression, to cast loose from the shore, and is also used of striking tents and breaking up a camp. We have the corresponding noun in 2 Tim. 4 : 6, "the time of my departure is at hand." The verb is found only here and in Luke 12 : 36. **And to be with Christ.** "'To depart' had always been a wish of the saints, but the idea of being with Christ belongs only to the New Testament." (Bengel.) These two ideas must be closely connected. "For death of itself will never be desired, because such a desire is at variance with natural feeling." (Calvin.)

[1] The preposition ἐκ denotes the origin, the source, of his embarrassment.

[2] That would require the genitive of the article τοῦ before the infinitive.

24 Nevertheless to abide in the flesh *is* more needful for you.
25 And having this confidence, I know that I shall abide and continue with you all for your furtherance and joy of faith;

24 better: yet to abide in the flesh is more need-
25 ful for your sake. And having this confidence, I know that I shall abide, yea, and abide with you

"Death is not a good, but it is a good after our departure to be with Christ." (Chrysostom.) The immediate connection of these words with 'to depart' shows that Paul did not conceive the intermediate state to be a condition of unconsciousness, but a far higher and more blessed existence than this earthly life, a state of conscious and intimate communion with Christ, beyond anything known on earth, although, as we collect from other passages, it is not the full and perfect fruition of a Christian's joy and reward. In this intermediate state the soul is bodiless (2 Cor. 5:8), and not until the resurrection of the body will our redemption be complete (Rom. 8:23); but, even with this drawback, the state of the Christian between death and the judgment is an advance upon our earthly condition. **Which is far better**—literally, *by far more better*, the original being an emphatic double comparative. Paul could scarcely have said this about the state after death, unless he viewed it as a conscious, active, progressive existence. Who can believe that if he had looked on death as the beginning of a long sleep, he would have had any such struggle to decide the question what to choose! With his active, energetic nature, and his intense desire to glorify his Master, he would undoubtedly have instantly chosen life, with all its ills, were death only a sleep; but death, in his view, will bring him nearer to his Saviour; to die is to be with Christ, and this unspeakable blessing renders him more than willing to go whenever the word of release shall be spoken. Socrates called death a removal to another place ("Apologia," 32), but Paul says it is to be with Christ. How much more glorious the outlook of the Christian apostle than that of the heathen philosopher! The apostle had a positive and most blessed conception of the future world, but how sad, because so uncertain, the closing words of the famous "Apology": "Now it is time to depart—I to die, you to live; and which of us is going to the better destiny is known only to the Deity."

24. In the preceding verse Paul has stated what he conceives to be best for himself; now he declares what is more needful for them. Instead of saying to stay is *better* for you, he changes the form of expression, and says **more needful,** as if his first expression had been "departure is needful for me." His departure was indeed a necessity, in so far as it alone would satisfy his desire for communion with Christ; but his stay on earth is a necessity which springs from the needs of others, and to this the first must give way. "It is more important for me to serve you than to enjoy heaven sooner. Heaven will not fail me." (Bengel.) The verb signifies "to stay on," stronger than the simple verb. (Rom. 16:1.) 'In the flesh' (ἐν τῇ σαρκί); the article is in place as referring to his own individual existence, but above (22), when he speaks of life in the body in a general way, he omits the article (ἐν σαρκί). **For you.** Of course, the Philippians would understand that this was not meant to apply exclusively to them, but included others besides.

25. The knowledge that his stay on earth is a necessity leads to the firm conviction that he is to abide here yet a while. **And having this confidence;** namely, that my remaining is needful. **I know**—not to be taken absolutely, but merely as expressing his conviction. In his address to the Ephesian elders at Miletus, he utters with equal assurance his conviction that he shall see their faces no more (Acts 20:25); yet if the conviction here expressed of his release and return to Philippi was realized, he probably did see their faces again. See 2 Tim. 4:20. But we need not trouble ourselves to harmonize such utterances with the actual facts, for in such matters Paul was left to the same means of knowledge as ourselves. See Acts 20:22. The verb "continue with" differs from the simple verb, which means "to remain." (Herodotus 1, 30; Plato, "Crito" 51 E; "Phaedo," 115 D.) **For your furtherance and joy of faith**—the purpose of his remaining, unfolding the thought contained in the words "more needful for you." (Ver. 24.) This is a part of that 'fruit' (ver. 22), for the sake of which he is willing to live. The word 'faith,' belongs to both 'further-

26 That your rejoicing may be more abundant in Jesus Christ for me by my coming to you again.
27 Only let your conversation be as it becometh the gospel of Christ: that whether I come and see you, or else be absent, I may hear of your affairs, that ye stand fast in one spirit, with one mind striving together for the faith of the gospel:

26 all, for your progress and joy [1] in the faith; that
your glorying may abound in Christ Jesus in me
27 through my presence with you again. Only [2] let
your manner of life be worthy of the gospel of Christ;
that, whether I come and see you or am absent, I
may hear of your state, that ye stand fast in one
spirit, with one soul striving [3] for the faith of the

1 Or, *of faith*......2 Gr. *behave as citizens worthily*......3 Gr. *with.*

ance' and 'joy'; their 'faith' has in it elements both of progress and joy, which his presence among them will promote.

26. This verse contains a still further expansion of the thought 'more needful for you' (ver. 24), bringing out still more clearly the purpose of his remaining. **Rejoicing.** The word means, properly, "matter of boasting" (καύχημα), not act of boasting or glorying (καύχησις), as in Rom. 4:2, "whereof to glory." See 1 Cor. 9:15; 2 Cor. 1:14. This matter of boasting is the possession of the gospel, and their state as Christians. Hence, the idea is that they may obtain a larger and richer increase of that which is their true glory and boast, the possession of the gospel and of the privileges of the Christian life. **In Christ Jesus for me**—better, *in me*, as in Revised Version. The parallelism 'in Christ, in me' is suggestive. They can obtain this increase only in Christ primarily, although it is to be in Paul, secondarily, by means of his renewed activity among them. By his coming again to them he would impart to them an increased measure of that whereof they boasted, but he would do this in the strength of Christ, so that to him must the glory of the work be ascribed.

In these last six verses Paul reveals some of the deepest and holiest aspirations of his soul, and surely nothing gives us a higher idea of his character than to behold him perplexed and uncertain on such a question, whether it were better to die and go to be with Christ, or to live and labor on awhile longer for the sake of increasing that fruit of his labors which he had already gathered so abundantly. It is only a superior spirit that could hesitate to choose between life and death; but even in this hesitation not a trace of self appears. If he thinks of death, it is of Christ he thinks; if he thinks of life, it is of his work he thinks; but in either case the thought of self is wholly forgotten.

1:27-2:11. EXHORTATION TO UNITY, HUMILITY, AND UNSELFISHNESS ENFORCED BY AN APPEAL TO THE EXAMPLE OF CHRIST.—The apostle urges them to be steadfast and united, like a band of Christian athletes (27); and to face their enemies with perfect fearlessness (28), remembering their high calling (29), and his own similar experiences (30).

27. Only—this is all I ask. Compare Gal. 2:10; 5:13. This exhortation to act worthily of the gospel of Christ involves all the obligations of the Christian life. Compare Eph. 4:1, seq. **Let your conversation**—better, *manner of life* (Revised Version). The verb means, primarily, to perform the duties of a citizen; so that the literal translation would be that of the margin of the Revised Version, "Only behave as citizens worthily of the gospel." Paul, however, has no reference to the political duties of the Philippians, but to their religious duties as members of the great commonwealth of heaven. His ordinary word for Christian conduct is 'walk,' but here he changes the figure to indicate more clearly the idea of those mutual duties which they owe each other as members of the heavenly commonwealth. He uses the corresponding noun in 3:20, and the verb in his speech before the Sanhedrim (Acts 23:1), but not elsewhere. **That whether I come,**[1] etc. Paul's uncertainty as to the future emerges here again. He knows not certainly whether he shall come and see them or not, but hope evidently predominates, as is hinted at in the order of the two alternatives—**come and see you, or else be absent.**

I may hear that ye stand fast. The verb does not itself signify to stand *fast*, but simply to *stand*, the idea of steadfastness

1 The structure of the sentence in the Greek is intelligible, but inexact, as if the writer had begun in one way and finished in another. He begins as if he were about to say, "whether coming and seeing, or being absent and hearing, I may know of your state"; but before he finishes he changes the construction, as if he had already written, "whether coming I may see," and therefore ends, "or being absent I may hear."

28 And in nothing terrified by your adversaries: which is to them an evident token of perdition, but to you of salvation, and that of God.
29 For unto you it is given in the behalf of Christ, not only to believe on him, but also to suffer for his sake;

28 gospel; and in nothing affrighted by the adversaries: which is for them an evident token of perdition, but of your salvation, and that from God;
29 because to you it hath been granted in the behalf of Christ, not only to believe on him, but also to suffer

coming from the context. **In one spirit, with one mind** (or, *soul*). The first refers to the higher part of our immaterial nature, that in which the Holy Spirit resides and works; the second refers to the lower part, the seat of the emotions and affections. The Philippians are exhorted to be united in their 'spirit,' in their holiest aspirations and convictions, and in their 'soul,' their affections, and sympathies. Of course, this can only be affected by the Holy Spirit. The words "with one soul" are connected with the following. **Striving together.** A metaphor from the athletic games. That which they are to co-operate for is **the faith of the gospel.** The absence of the connecting article blends these two words into a single idea, gospel faith; that is, the substance of the apostolic teaching. Compare Jude 3. This faith of the gospel is the one thing they must most jealously guard and defend.

28. In nothing terrified by your adversaries. It is not enough to be united in spirit, but they must exhibit an unflinching courage. The original word for 'terrified,' found only here in the New Testament, is very strong, describing, primarily, the terror of a frightened animal. 'Adversaries.' As these were well known to his readers, the apostle does not describe them, so that we are in the dark about them; but as their hostility was similar to that from which Paul himself suffered at Philippi (ver. 30), it is probably some outbreak of the heathen populace to which he has reference. But however numerous or powerful their adversaries are, the Philippians ought to face them fearlessly. All these enemies can do is to scare them, and the Philippians ought not to let them succeed even in this. "He that feareth God need fear none else." **Which**[1]—that is, your fearlessness, referring back not to any single word, but to the idea suggested by the previous admonition. **An evident token of perdition.** Their courage becomes a proof of their enemies' destruction, by clearly revealing the divine source of their own superior strength. These Christians are shown to be helped of God by the wonderful bravery they display. Their enemies are, therefore, fighting against God, and nothing but destruction awaits them. The cowardice of the Philippians would, on the contrary, bring the gospel into contempt and confirm opposers in their hardness and blindness of heart. **But,** on the other hand, this fearlessness is to you a token of **salvation** for the same reason that it is a token of the 'perdition' of their foes, because it reveals God's presence and power. Compare 2 Thess. 1 : 4, seq., where the faith and patience of the Thessalonians are described as a proof of the righteous judgment of God, the result of which would be their salvation. **And that of God.** This fearlessness, which is a token both of their own salvation and of their enemies' destruction, is from God; it is not a natural characteristic, but a divine omen of victory. Calvin beautifully suggests that these words were added, "that the taste of the grace of God may allay the bitterness of the cross."

29. This verse confirms the last words of the preceding verse, 'and that of God.' **For unto you it is given**—literally, *granted as a favor;* that is, by God. It is a proof of the divine favor that you are called into trials where such fearlessness is required. Compare Acts 5 : 4. 'Unto you' is emphatic by position. God has conferred upon *you* this privilege, as he has not upon all other believers. 'Is given'—strictly, *was given,* referring to the time when their Christian life began. **In the behalf of Christ.**[2] It is not an ab-

[1] *Since it is* is the proper force of the pronoun ἥτις. It refers logically to the whole clause, but agrees grammatically with its predicate by a common attraction. (Winer, p. 166. Compare Eph. 3 : 13.)

[2] We have here again, in the Greek, a slightly irregular sentence. Paul began the sentence as if he were about to write, "for to you it was given in behalf of Christ to suffer"; but before he added the words "to suffer" he bethinks him of the necessary antecedent of all sacrifice "faith," and therefore he proceeds "not only *to* believe on him, but also to suffer for his sake"; so that the phrase "in behalf of Christ," which he had written with the first form of the sentence in mind, is in part superfluous. To make the sentence perfectly regular we should have to strike it out, and put Christ in place of "him" in the next clause.

30 Having the same conflict which ye saw in me, and now hear *to be* in me.

30 in his behalf: having the same conflict which ye saw in me, and now hear to be in me.

CHAPTER II.

IF *there be* therefore any consolation in Christ, if any comfort of love, if any fellowship of the Spirit, if any bowels and mercies,

1 If there is therefore any exhortation in Christ, if any consolation of love, if any fellowship of the

stract truth, in which they believe and for which they suffer, but the personal Christ. On him they believe, for him they suffer. Suffering for Christ Paul declares to be a special grace, because, when rightly endured, it works out the believer's sanctification. (Rom. 5:3, seq.) Paul looks beyond the malice of enemies, and beholds in their efforts the divine favor toward his suffering people. He writes out of his own experience, when he speaks of the double grace of believing and suffering (see 2 Cor. 11:23, seq.); and hence, words that from almost any other lips might have seemed bitter irony, became freighted with the strength and comfort that only likeness of experience can impart.

30. The experience of the Philippians is expressly compared with his own. A part of this experience they had only heard of in his letters; but a part of it had passed under their very eyes, when, on his first visit to Philippi, he was scourged and cast into prison, and his feet confined in the stocks. The indignity of this treatment Paul seems never to have forgotten. He speaks with intense indignation about it in his First Epistle to the Thessalonians. (2:2.) Compare, also, Acts 16:16, seq., where Luke's language seems to reflect the apostle's deep and intense feelings. It is probable that in some similar outbreak of heathen violence, the Philippians had themselves suffered in a like manner, and Paul seems to refer to such an experience in 2 Cor. 8:2, where he speaks of the churches of Macedonia having had a "great trial (proof) of affliction." What delicacy of feeling the apostle shows in thus comparing the Philippians with himself, and how naturally the comparison would stimulate them to exhibit the same spirit of patience, courage, and cheerfulness which they had beheld in him! Bengel, on the words "in me," adds the comment, beautifully suggestive of their implied significance, "in me who am not terrified." The unwritten admonition to copy his example, suggested by the twice-repeated "in me," could not fail to speak directly to their hearts.

Ch. 2. CONTINUATION OF THE EXHORTATION WHICH EXTENDS FROM 1:27–2:11.—The apostle returns from the slight digression in 1:28–30 to the topic of the unity of the Philippians; which he urges in a most tender and persuasive manner (1, 2), joining with the plea for unity an appeal also for humility (3) and unselfishness (4), and enforcing his whole admonition by a noble and eloquent description of the example of Jesus Christ (5–11).

1. If there be therefore any consolation (better, *exhortation*) **in Christ.** 'If there be' implies no doubt of the existence of the following motives, but is simply a tender form of appeal to what is well known to exist. The word translated 'consolation' in the Common Version has the general signification of "encouragement," "exhortation," though it is sometimes used in the more limited sense of "comfort," "consolation." Here the context decides for the wider meaning, since the next word conveys specifically the idea of consolation. Compare 1 Cor. 14:3. For the corresponding verbs similarly joined together, compare 1 Thess. 2:11. This 'exhortation' is in Christ; that is, it is Christian exhortation, a practical manifestation of the life that flows from Christ. **If any comfort of love**—comfort which springs from love as its source. Compare 2 Cor. 1:3–7 for a beautiful illustration of this comfort of love. **If any fellowship of the Spirit**—participation in the gifts and graces of the Spirit, the basis of all true unity. Compare 2 Cor. 13:14. **If any bowels and mercies**—any tender and affectionate yearnings and compassions. The two words are sometimes joined into a single idea, 'bowels of mercies,' as in Col. 3:12; and in Hebrew a single word (רַחֲמִים) combines the meanings of both, kindness, affection (σπλάγ-

2 Fulfil ye my joy, that ye be likeminded, having the same love, *being* of one accord, of one mind.
3 *Let* nothing *be done* through strife or vainglory; but in lowliness of mind let each esteem other better than themselves.

2 Spirit, if any tender mercies and compassions, fulfil
ye my joy, that ye be of the same mind, having
the same love, being of one accord,[1] of one mind;
3 *doing* nothing through faction or through vainglory, but in lowliness of mind each counting other

1 Some ancient authorities read *of the same mind.*

χνα, οἰκτιρμοί)[1] and pity, compassion. This kind and compassionate affection springs from the 'fellowship of the Spirit,' while the 'exhortation in Christ' produces 'comfort of love.' Thus we have in the fourfold division of this verse a reference to unity with Christ, and the spiritual result, and also to unity with the Spirit, and its spiritual result. These considerations are so many arguments why the Philippians should hasten to complete his happiness by a perfect exhibition of unity. The language of his appeal is made unusually tender and impressive by the fourfold repetition of the words 'if any.' "Persuasion herself could not speak more persuasively."

2. Fulfil ye my joy. Compare John 3:29. Already the apostle had joy in the state of the Philippian Church, but he wished that joy made full, complete, by their perfect unanimity of spirit. This unanimity he describes by several phrases which vary but slightly from each other. They are to **be likeminded**—that is, to think the same thing, to have **the same love**—and finally, to be **of one accord, of one mind**—with perfect unity of soul to think one thing. The first and last of these three expressions do not differ essentially. In Greek, as in English, both are sometimes joined together, "one and the same thing." But that which adds a new suggestion to the last clause is rather the word translated in Common Version and Revised Version 'being of one accord' (σύμψυχοι). This word should be closely connected with what follows, and the whole translated: *having the same love, with harmony of soul, thinking one thing.* They should not merely direct their minds to the same thoughts, but should do this in complete harmony. They might think about the same thing only to contend and dispute, but Paul wishes them to think harmoniously about it, to dwell upon that view of it on which they are agreed, and if there should be any diversity of opinion, to wait, as he afterward enjoins them (3:15), for God's fuller revelations to decide the case. The second of the three clauses adds to the duty of likemindedness that of mutual love, for as Chrysostom says: "There is such a thing as being likeminded, and yet not having love." Their oneness must be of heart and mind both.

3. Let nothing be done through strife or vainglory. Instead of supplying the verb 'let,' as in the Common Version, it is better to carry forward the participle from the last verse, *thinking nothing in the way of strife or of vain glory.* (Winer, p. 587.) The word 'strife' has appeared already (1:15); the second word 'vainglory' does not occur elsewhere in the New Testament, though in Gal. 5:26 we have the adjective 'vainglorious.' See Revised Version. These two, strife and the spirit of display, destroy unity in the church. "For both diseases he brings forward one remedy—humility." (Calvin.) **But in lowliness of mind.** According to Greek usage the names of the various virtues have the article. Hence, 'lowliness' has the article in the Greek, signifying the virtue of *humility.* The Greek word for 'lowliness' is one of the words which Christianity has coined. The nearest classical Greek word signifies "meanness of spirit." To think lightly of one's self was never a virtue in the eyes of a Greek. It was only justifiable, as Aristotle says, when one had no reason for thinking otherwise. That any one of great powers should be "meek and lowly in heart" never suggested itself to the Greek as possible. In fact, his supreme virtue was high-mindedness, or, as Aristotle puts it, "the

[1] We must call attention to the curious ungrammatical use of τις before the two nouns σπλάγχνα and οἰκτιρμοί. The manuscript evidence is entirely in favor of this reading, but on account of its ungrammatical character most commentators have preferred the reading τινα. There seems, however, no reason why, if τινα were the original reading, it should ever have been changed, while it would have been perfectly natural for some copyist to alter the strange and anomalous τις. Tischendorf says we must preserve the reading τις, unless we prefer to act as grammarians rather than as editors. Alford's explanation of its use seems plausible, that as the two Greek nouns represent a single Hebrew noun רַחֲמִים, they were regarded as expressing but a single idea, and the singular pronoun was used instead of the plural.

4 Look not every man on his own things, but every man also on the things of others.
5 Let this mind be in you, which was also in Christ Jesus:
6 Who, being in the form of God, thought it not robbery to be equal with God:

4 better than himself; not looking each of you to his
own things, but each of you also to the things of
5 others. Have this mind in you, which was also in
6 Christ Jesus: who existing in the form of God,
counted not the being on an equality with God a

deeming oneself worthy of greatness, because worthy." And Heine reveals this same instinct of human nature in modern times when he speaks contemptuously of the "dog's virtue of humility." The New Testament writers had therefore to coin a word for this Christian grace of humility.

Let each esteem others better than themselves. "That may be done not only outwardly, but by true humility, when a man, through seld-denial, turns his eyes away from his own privileges, and steadily contemplates another's endowments in which he is superior." (Bengel.) Compare Rom. 12:10; Eph. 5:21; 1 Peter 5:5.

4. Look not every man on his own things, but every man also, etc. In the Greek there is no period at the close of ver. 3, but the sentence continues, and is properly translated in the Revised Version "not looking." These words contain a warning against selfishness, following appropriately on the exhortation to 'lowliness,' for pride and selfishness grow out of the same root. In the second clause the word 'also' modifies the exclusiveness of the first assertion, suggesting that some consideration of one's own things must be allowed. The apostle had first said, 'look not upon his own things,' but by this word 'also' he softens his extreme injunction, and allows their own things some regard. Without such a modification his injunction would have passed beyond reasonable limits. (Winer, p. 498.)[1] The words of the apostle (ver. 2-4) seem to intimate that there were those in the Philippian Church who were lacking in the graces of humility and unselfishness. They overestimated their own services and excellencies, and depreciated their brethren. No division in doctrine is here suggested, but the danger —it is perhaps nothing more—of a possible estrangement of heart and the disruption of their previous good fellowship through this excess of pride on the part of some.

5-11. The apostle now enforces his admonition to unity, humility, and unselfishness, by the example of Jesus Christ (5), who did not regard his own prerogatives or position (6), but sacrificed them for the sake of others (7), yea, went to the very depths of humiliation and shame (8), on which account God the Father has most highly exalted him (9), that the whole creation may recognize his glory (10), and own his rule (11).

This passage, the only doctrinal one in our Epistle, is one of the most important in all Paul's writings, and the most complete statement of Christ's exalted rank to be found anywhere outside of the Gospel of John. Its importance justifies and requires a more extended examination.

5. Let this mind be in you (or, *think ye this in yourselves*)—that is, *in your hearts.* Compare Matt. 9:3, 4. **Which was also in Christ Jesus**—literally, *which was also thought in Christ Jesus.* 'Also' refers to the similarity of disposition between Christ and his followers: in you as *also* in Christ. The name Christ Jesus refers to the Saviour in his entire existence, pre-incarnate and incarnate, not that he was ever known by this name until born in the flesh, but Paul could describe him in no other way so clearly as by this well-known historical name. The context shows that the apostle includes Christ's entire existence under this name, and not merely his earthly life, as some have supposed, for ver. 6 evidently refers to his pre-incarnate state, and the incarnate state is not touched upon till ver. 7. John used the word Logos to describe the Saviour previous to his earthly life, but Paul has nowhere used that word.

6. Who, being in the form of God. 'Being' is not the participle of the substantive verb *to be*, but comes from a stronger verb and means *subsisting, existing.* 'Form' (μορφή) is not the same as nature (φύσις οὐσία), but designates in man his external appearance; hence in the Divine Being it must describe what corresponds to our external appearance, that through which the divine presence manifests itself. God, who is a Spirit, reveals himself

[1] The plural, ἕκαστοι, is found nowhere else in the New Testament.

in his glory, which the apostle here calls appropriately the 'form of God.' The 'form of God' is not therefore the Godhead, although as Bengel well observes, "He who existed in the 'form of God,' is God." Paul is led to use this word, because he is thinking of what Christ laid aside. Christ did not and could not lay aside his Godhead, but he did lay aside his divine glory, or form. Compare Col. 1: 15, "image," and Heb. 1: 3, "express image." **Thought it not robbery.** The word translated 'robbery' in the Common Version, and 'a prize' in the Revised Version, is the chief stumbling block in the interpretation of this passage, and the explanation hinges mainly upon the meaning we give this one word. It is a very rare word in the Greek language, occurring but once in profane literature, and not more than two or three times in ecclesiastical literature, and there probably as an echo of this passage. The determination of its meaning is therefore very difficult. According to grammatical usage, by its termination, it denotes an action, that is, the act of seizing, or seizure. Nouns of the same termination very often, however, are used to express the result of an action, instead of the action itself. In determining, therefore, the meaning of any single word its form is not decisive. Usage alone can decide. When usage fails to clear up the meaning, the context of the passage must be the last resort. If in this case we turn to usage, the evidence is of course very slight, but what there is sustains the meaning suggested by the termination of the word. Plutarch, in his "Morals," uses the word of the custom of seizing or kidnapping children from Crete. Interpreters have generally, however, given the passive meaning to this word on the ground that nouns with a termination, such as generally denote an action, are often used like those with the termination that denote a result. This is undoubtedly often the case, as noted above, but we have no right to assume that *any* noun of the former class may be so used, but must furnish incontestable evidence of some example of such usage, before we are justified in neglecting the obvious significance for a less natural one, especially if the obvious meaning suits the context just as well. Now there is no occasion from the context to alter that significance of this word, which we obtain by observing its form and Plutarch's use of it. Christ, for instance, did not consider his equality with God a robbery or seizure, that is, he did not view his exalted position as a means of seizing to himself the glory and the exaltation which he afterward acquired. Compare 1 Tim. 6: 5, where Paul speaks of certain ones who supposed godliness to be gain, that is, evidently a *means* of gain. So Christ might have regarded his Godhead as a means of appropriating the glory he now wears. He might have come to earth in all the splendor of Deity, to win the homage of human hearts. But, instead of that, he looked not on his own things —he laid aside his divine glory, and appeared in the form of a servant, and in the way of humiliation and self-denial reached his present elevation. Thus the context admits this meaning of the word, and if that be so, there can be no just reason for assuming an unusual signification for which no example has been cited.

We must, however, admit that this interpretation has few advocates. Meyer proposed it, and has been followed by Alford alone outside of Germany, and by but very few German scholars. The generally accepted interpretation gives to this word the passive meaning of "things seized." Those who assign this meaning reach in general the same result as that proposed above, but naturally and logically their interpretation brings forth a Socinian view of the passage. For if we adopt the passive meaning of the word, then we are taught that Christ did not think equality with God a thing to be seized, hence of course equality with God was not already his own. To obviate this difficulty, the exact meaning of "things seized" is changed to "things retained or held fast," and so the same result is reached as in our interpretation, but by making two arbitrary changes in the significance of the word.

The shade given by the words 'thought not' should not be overlooked. Paul might have said: He did not make equality with God a robbery, but he added the words above quoted to indicate that he did not for one moment even *contemplate* the possibility of such a thing, much less attempt to put it into execution. These words, therefore, answer to the 'look not' of ver. 4. The Philippians are enjoined to renounce the selfish consideration of their own rights, prerogatives, claims, etc., and to enforce this, they are told that Christ

7 But made himself of no reputation, and took upon him the form of a servant, and was made in the likeness of men:
8 And being found in fashion as a man, he humbled himself, and became obedient unto death, even the death of the cross.

7 thing to be grasped, but emptied himself, taking the form of a [1] servant, [2] being made in the likeness of
8 men; and being found in fashion as a man, he humbled himself, becoming obedient *even* unto death,

1 Or, *bondservant*......2 Gr. *becoming in.*

allowed no thought of the selfish use of his position to enter his mind.[1]

To be equal with God. This is not essentially different from 'being in the form of God,' but describes the same idea from another side. It describes Christ's existence as an existing in an equal way with God. The adverb equal (ἴσα), not the noun (ἴσος), is used. With the latter Christ's equality of essence would have been referred to, but there is a singular propriety in the use of the adverb instead of the noun, because it was not his equal nature, but his equal mode of existence that he laid aside. Thus Paul has chosen the phrases 'form of God' and 'equal mode of existence' with singular felicity. These and these alone could be held fast, or abandoned. Equality of nature must be permanent.

To sum up now the meaning of this verse: Christ, who in his antemundane state was in 'the form of God,' who was "the image of the invisible God," "the brightness of his glory, and the express image of his person" (Heb. 1:3), did not consider this equality with God a means of seizure, or self-enrichment, did not make use of that form, and manifest that glory, appearing in all the splendor of Deity to win his present state of glory and honor; but, as we are told subsequently, took a very different way, the way of humility and self-abasement.

7. But made himself of no reputation —better, literally, *emptied himself* (Revised Version); that is, of that form, that peculiar manifestation of the divine glory. He not only did not make this form a means of self-glorification, but did the very opposite—renounced all his glorious prerogatives, and became a servant. 'Himself' is emphatic by its position in the Greek, and thus invites attention to the divine subject who disrobed himself. **And took upon him the form of a servant.** The 'and' should be omitted, and the sentence read 'taking,' etc. (Revised Version), showing how the emptying was realized. He put off the form of God, and put on 'the form of a servant'—that is, a servant of God, not of man. 'Form' differs from 'fashion' (ver. 8) by describing what is more essential, 'fashion' referring to what is more external and changeable. The two verbs, formed from these two nouns, are brought into an instructive connection in Rom. 12:2. In ch. 3:21 we have a verb and adjective formed from the two nouns brought together. The taking of a servant's form is now explained: **Being made in the likeness of men.** 'The form of a servant' was 'the likeness of men.' The 'and' of the Common Version is again unnecessary. 'Likeness' differs from both 'form' and 'fashion,' being more subordinate than the former, and less than the latter. He was 'made in the likeness of men,' not that he was not strictly and truly man, but that he was something more, the God-man, the "Word made flesh." "He was not only soul and body, but God and soul and body." (Theodoret.) Compare Rom. 8:3, "in the likeness of sinful flesh," where the phrase suggests similarity and dissimilarity; flesh like our own, but sinless, not sinful flesh.

8. And being found in fashion as a man. Paul now proceeds to describe a deeper depth still in this emptying process, but he first repeats again the idea of Christ's humanity by the words 'being found in fashion as a man,' where we see again how carefully the apostle guards his thought. Christ was found as a man in fashion—that is, in bearing, manner, gestures, speech, dress. In all these respects he was like other men. Yet the thought that he was not merely a man moulds the expression into this peculiar form. Before (ver. 6), Paul used the strongest language concerning Christ's pre-existence, 'subsisting, in the form of God'; here and in ver. 7, with an evident feeling of the peculiar character of Christ's humanity, a humanity wholly unique, he says:

1 The aorist (ἡγήσατο) refers to the moment when he left heaven, and conceives of him as then putting the thought aside.

'being made in *the likeness* of men,' and 'being found in fashion *as* a man.' The 'and' at the beginning of the verse connects the verbs 'emptied' (ver. 7), and 'humbled' (ver. 8). See Revised Version. To the putting aside of divine powers and prerogatives is now added the further step of humbling himself in that new mode of existence. "The state of emptying gradually becomes deeper." (Bengel.) Had Christ appeared as a second Solomon in all the glory of earthly royalty, he would still have emptied himself of that greater glory which he had with the Father before the world was (John 18:5); but he descended through all the ranks of humanity, until he reached the lowest, yea, until he appeared as the vilest, as a criminal, a malefactor. The verb 'humbled' is placed before the pronoun in the Greek, thus reversing the order in ver. 7, because there the glorious subject of the emptying process was to be made prominent; here the wonderful act of humiliation. **And became obedient.** The 'and' is again superfluous. Render 'becoming obedient' (Revised Version)—that is, unto God, not to man. As one who had taken a creature's place and position, the Son must become obedient, and this obedience he rendered in full, although it led to a most shameful death. **Unto death, even the death of the cross.** He was obedient unto the very extremity of obedience, death, although that death came in the most disgraceful form, upon the cross. The cross was a mode of punishment used only for slaves by the Romans, and among the Jews regarded as entailing a curse. (Gal. 3:13; Heb. 12:2.) The death of Christ is not here considered as an atonement, for that view of it did not come within the scope of the apostle's immediate purpose, but it is viewed solely as an example of perfect obedience. "To live as man was self-surrender; to die as man was self-sacrifice—the deepest of humility, the highest of obedience." Compare Rom. 5:19; Heb. 5:8; Matt. 26:39.

It may be well at this point to give a brief summary of the different interpretations of this important passage. In general two lines of interpretation have been followed. The first class of commentators have understood the whole passage to refer to Christ's earthly life. He, while on earth, did not arrogate to himself divine honors, and did not display fully his divine powers, but concealed his divinity. This view has been advocated by able commentators, among others Neander and Luther. But the interpretation halts in many particulars. Christ on earth was never in the form of God, and if the apostle had wished to express the idea, that he renounced divine honors and concealed his glorious rank, the natural way to have done so with these words would have been: "Who being equal with God thought it not robbery to be in the form of God;" for the 'form' must be the glory that was hidden and suppressed. But this is the very reverse of what the apostle actually says. Again, 'taking the form of a servant' cannot mean Christ's lowly condition, because the following clause plainly describes it as becoming man.

The second class of interpreters recognize a reference to the two states of Christ's existence, the pre-incarnate and the incarnate, in ver. 6, 7, finding the earthly existence first described in ver. 7. But beyond this there are the widest divergencies of opinion on other points. Many, taking the equality with God to be something different from the form of God, declare that Christ did not grasp at this higher position of divine equality, but came to earth and won by obedience that place which he now holds at the Father's side. This interpretation,[1] however, is out of harmony with the context, and is not a correct exegesis of the passage. From the context we see that Paul is teaching humility and unselfishness, and to enforce the lesson he quotes the example of Christ, who, according to this view, did not arrogate Deity or equality with God. But where is the pertinency of the illustration? The Philippians are not to regard their own

[1] The order of words in the Greek is opposed to this view. Had Paul intended to declare that while Christ possessed 'the form of God,' he did not arrogate to himself 'equality with God,' he would naturally have given the place of emphasis to the words 'equal with God.' Being in the form of God he did not think *equality with God* a thing to be seized. The actual emphasis in the text is, however, on the word seizure or robbery, showing that he did not make a *seizure* of his equality with God—that is, did not use it to seize upon the honors he now wears.

9 Wherefore God also hath highly exalted him, and given him a name which is above every name:
10 That at the name of Jesus every knee should bow, of *things* in heaven, and *things* in earth, and *things* under the earth;

9 yea, the death of the cross. Wherefore also God highly exalted him, and gave unto him the name
10 which is above every name; that in the name of Jesus every knee should bow, of *things* in heaven and *things* on earth and [1] *things* under the earth,

1 Or, things *of the world below.*

things—that is, honors, prerogatives, etc.—because Christ did not claim what was *not* his own! Surely there was no particular humility and unselfishness in not seizing upon something that did not belong to him. To have arrogated equality with God when he did not possess it, would have been the height of impious presumption. In order to give us a pertinent illustration, Paul must present Christ as not looking on his own things. A correct exegesis of the passages shows this to be the nature of the illustration; Christ did not look upon his own—that is, his equality with God—but surrendered it, emptying himself and assuming a human form, and so becoming a most impressive example of humility and unselfishness. He might have acted otherwise. He might have arrogated to himself all the honors that he now wears. He might have displayed his godhead and majesty as a means of glorifying himself, but instead of so doing—and herein he becomes a wonderful example for us—he looked not at his own things, dismissed them from his mind, and thought only of the things of others, of humanity and its great needs, and, emptying himself of his divine majesty and glory, he appeared on earth in the lowliest condition of life, a Galilean peasant, companion of illiterate fishermen, friend of publicans and sinners. Thus he thought not of his divine rank as a means of seizure, but drew the world to himself by the "cords of a man," and became the magnet to attract the hearts of all by becoming the world's sacrifice.

9. Paul proceeds now to the subject of the Saviour's exaltation, which includes ver. 9-11. Compare Eph. 1 : 20-23. **Wherefore**—in consequence of this course of humility and obedience. **God hath also**—better, *also God* (Revised Version), the also belonging to all that follows and connecting God's act of exaltation with Christ's act of humiliation. **Highly exalted.** This is one of Paul's peculiarly expressive compounds. "A noble compound verb." (Bengel.) Compounds formed by the preposition for 'over' above (ὑπέρ) are especially frequent in his epistles. See Rom. 5 : 20; 7 : 13; 1 Cor. 12 : 31; 2 Cor. 10 : 14; Eph. 3 : 20, and elsewhere. The exaltation here referred to is Christ's elevation to the right hand of God, his investiture as King of saints, with full power, dominion, and glory. The glory which Christ willingly resigned he has received again with greater fullness than ever. **And given him a name**—in fulfillment of the divine law which Christ himself enunciated. (Luke 14 : 11; 18 : 14.) In place of the name which he bore on earth, a name so often spoken with contempt and scorn, God has given him a most glorious name. This is but another way of saying that God has made him who was once despised most honorable. Many have discussed the question what the name of Christ in his glory might be, but it seems unnecessary to take the words so literally. We have no reason to suppose the Saviour's actual name in heaven to be anything different from his name on earth, but while on earth it was despised, it is now honored and destined to be honored universally. That Jesus still bears his earthly name we are almost forced to conclude from the words which follow in ver. 10.

10. The purpose of the exaltation of Jesus is expressed in this and the following verse; namely, that to him may be paid the profoundest homage of the entire universe. **At the name** should rather be *in the name* (Revised Version). It corresponds precisely in meaning to the "in my name," which Jesus himself makes the condition of acceptable prayer. (John 14 : 13, 14; 15 : 16; 16 : 23, 24, 26.) Our Lord declares that in his name the disciples shall offer their prayers, and Paul simply expands the application of those words to a still wider sphere, and prophesies that in that same name of Jesus the whole creation shall offer its worship. Disciples now acknowledge the high worth of the name of Jesus in their prayers, but Paul carries us on to the more glorious acknowledgment of that name, when the whole universe shall bow its knee in the name of Jesus, that is, on account of what he is.

11 And *that* every tongue should confess that Jesus Christ *is* Lord, to the glory of God the Father.
12 Wherefore, my beloved, as ye have always obeyed, not as in my presence only, but now much more in my absence, work out your own salvation with fear and trembling:

11 and that every tongue should confess that Jesus Christ is Lord, to the glory of God the Father.
12 So then, my beloved, even as ye have always obeyed, not [1] as in my presence only, but now much more in my absence, work out your own salvation

1 Some ancient authorities omit *as*.

With such an interpretation of the passage, there is not the slightest justification of the ritualistic custom of bowing the head when the name of Jesus is spoken. **Every knee should bow** is a figurative description of the act of worship. Compare Rom. 11 : 4; 14 : 11; Eph. 3 : 14. It brings the scene vividly before the imagination, and suggests the vast throng in the natural attitude of adoration. Those who pay this worship are all created beings. The Common Version, and the Revised Version also, translate **things in heaven,** etc.; but though the Greek is ambiguous, the masculine form is undoubtedly in the apostle's mind, and the rendering should be "*of beings in heaven,*" etc. The beings in heaven are the angels, those in or on earth are living men, and those under the earth are the dead.

11. As there will be a universal expression of silent homage in the bowing of the knees, so there will be a universal expression of audible worship in the speaking voices of all created beings. **And that every tongue should confess.** The language is a reminiscence of Isaiah 45 : 23, which is quoted exactly in Rom. 14 : 11. Compare Rev. 5 : 13. **That Jesus Christ is Lord.** This is the exalted honor paid to the Saviour that the whole universe at last acknowledges his lordship. Not all will do this gladly and heartily, but some with love and some with fear; yet all must confess —openly and fully, as the Greek implies—the right of Christ to rule. Even those who have here said, "we will not have this man to reign over us," will then bow their knees in homage, and confess his authority. Observe how this idea of universality is emphasized by the thrice-repeated word 'every.' **To the glory of God the Father.** The exalted position of Christ does not in the least detract from the glory of the Father, but rather enhances it. The honor paid to Christ reflects glory upon the Father whose Son he is. The worship of the Son cannot be separated from the worship of the Father. In the beautiful vision of universal worship described in Rev. 5, all creatures are represented as ascribing "blessing and honour and glory and power unto him that sitteth upon the throne, and unto the Lamb, for ever and ever."

12-18. EXHORTATION TO PERFECT OBEDIENCE IN IMITATION OF THIS GREAT EXAMPLE OF JESUS CHRIST.—The apostle now resumes his exhortation in a form somewhat similar to the beginning of this course of thought in 1 : 27, urging the Philippians to work out (12) the salvation that has already been inwrought into their souls (13), keeping free from murmurings and dissensions (14), and so honoring God in the midst of a wicked world (15), and rewarding the apostle for his labors (16), who is ready to sacrifice his life, if necessary, for them (17), in which case they are even to rejoice (18).

12. Wherefore—because Christ has given us such an example of obedience. **As ye have always obeyed**—that is, God, not the apostle. In his wise and gracious way, Paul first compliments them on their past obedience, and then exhorts to a still more perfect obedience. **Not as in my presence only, but now much more in my absence.** In this and the following clause the thoughts are crowded and made somewhat obscure. Instead of saying "as ye have always obeyed in my presence, so continue to obey in my absence," the apostle substitutes for the words "continue to obey" the expressive phrase **work out your own salvation with fear and trembling,** transferring the mind instantly and forcibly to the result of such obedience, and then, instead of making a simple contrast between his presence and his absence, he blends with it the suggestion that the obedience should be much more earnest and complete in his absence; they are not to obey as they did in his presence, but 'much more' in his 'absence.' The thoughts are expressed with such brevity as to render the structure somewhat rugged and the exact sense

13 For it is God which worketh in you both to will and to do of *his* good pleasure.
14 Do all things without murmurings and disputings:

13 with fear and trembling; for it is God who worketh in you both to will and to work, for his good pleas-
14 ure. Do all things without murmurings and ques-

uncertain.[1] The obedience is suggested by the thought of Christ's obedience "unto death" (ver. 8), and the working out of salvation corresponds to the glorious reward that he obtained (ver. 9). The Philippians are exhorted to be more faithful and earnest in his absence, because they are now deprived of his help and there is a greater need of personal watchfulness and circumspection. Calvin well says: "It is the part of hypocrites to do well when in the sight of those by whom they wish to be approved, but to indulge in freedoms when removed from observation." What a rare church must that at Philippi have been, that Paul could say of them "as ye have always obeyed." Compare, also, 1 : 5, "from the first day until now." **Work out.** The compound verb expresses the idea of perseverance even to the end. This word gives no support to the notion that we can accomplish our own salvation; for in the next verse we are told that it is God that worketh in you. The believer can only co-operate with God in developing the life that God has first imparted. Without God there would be no beginning, and without him there would be no ending of the work. **Your own salvation.** 'Own' is inserted with emphasis. Each man must work out his *own* salvation. See Winer, p. 151. This should engage their thoughts rather than the vainglorious ambitions and selfish purposes against which he warned them in ver. 3 and 4. As Christ, by his obedience, secured the highest possible glory, so, by their obedience, they will secure their greatest reward, that is, salvation. **With fear and trembling.** These words occur only three times in Paul's epistles, and always in reference to obedience: 1 Cor. 2 : 3; 2 Cor. 7 : 15; Eph. 6 : 5. The fear is not exactly the fear of God, but of the greatness of the task and of the possibility of failure; trembling, the physical accompaniment of fear, is added to give fullness and completeness to the phrase, without suggesting any new thought. They are to exhibit the utmost solicitude lest they may not do enough to make their salvation secure. Compare 1 Cor. 10 : 12; Heb. 2 : 3.

13. For it is God. The apostle now expresses the encouraging motive to such careful obedience. The fact that God is the Author of salvation should encourage us to work out our salvation, for he will surely complete the work that he has begun (1 : 6), and it should produce fear and trembling, lest we displease him by our carelessness and negligence. **That worketh in you.** God begins the work of salvation by working in our hearts, and we carry that work out to its completion when by obedience we yield ourselves up to God. The life must first be implanted, wrought in us, before we can begin to work it out, to unfold and develop it. **To will and to do of his good pleasure.** To God is ascribed both the willing and the doing. This doing is not the same as that already enjoined upon men (ver. 12); that was described as 'working out,' carrying to the end (κατεργάζεσθε), this as 'working in' (ἐνεργεῖν)—the same word by which he has described God's work. God does not work in us the accomplishment of salvation, for that would leave man nothing to do, but he imparts to us the willing, the right choice, and the doing, the moral ability to carry out the dictates of the will. That carrying out is our own work. (Ver. 12.) "We will, but God works in us the willing; we work, but God works in us the working." (Augustine.) The theologians named these two divine operations, preventing and assisting grace. **Of his good pleasure**—rather *for, for the sake of;* that is, to satisfy his benevolent disposition. The reason of God's action is to be found in the promptings of his gracious will. It is "for the sake of his love." (Chrysostom.) Compare 1 Tim. 2 : 4.

14. Do all things. He here indicates the spirit in which the injunction of ver. 12 should be carried out, and recalls the previous admonitions to harmony and unity. (1 : 27; 2 : 2, seq.) 'All' is placed first in the Greek with emphasis. All that you do, do in the spirit of cheer-

[1] The Common Version seems to connect the words "not as in my presence," etc., with the preceding verbs; but the Greek negative would then have been οὐ, not μή. See Winer, p. 476.

15 That ye may be blameless and harmless, the sons of God, without rebuke, in the midst of a crooked and perverse nation, among whom ye shine as lights in the world;

16 Holding forth the word of life; that I may rejoice in the day of Christ, that I have not run in vain, neither laboured in vain.

15 tionings; that ye may become blameless and harmless, children of God without blemish in the midst
of a crooked and perverse generation, among whom
16 ye are seen as [1]lights in the world, holding forth
the word of life: that I may have whereof to glory
in the day of Christ, that I did not run in vain

[1] Gr. *luminaries.*

ful obedience. "It is better to do nothing than to do it with murmurings." (Chrysostom.) **Without murmurings and disputings.** The first is an onomatopoetic word, like the English word 'murmuring,' and refers to expressed complaints; the second denotes inward questionings. 'Disputings' suggests a rebellion of the thoughts against God, while 'murmurings' may spring merely from a bad state of heart; the first arise from a lack of faith, the second from a lack of love. There is no doubt allusion here to the conduct of the children of Israel in the wilderness, whose murmurings at that time became proverbial. (1 Cor. 10:10.) "The slave murmurs, but what son will murmur who, while about his father's work, works also for himself." (Chrysostom.)

15. The apostle here describes the high mark they are to aim at. **That ye may be** (rather, *become*)—indicating growth, development. **Blameless and harmless.** Compare in 1:10 the twofold description of moral righteousness, 'pure and without offence.' 'Blameless' refers to their character in the judgment of others; 'harmless'—literally, *unmixed, pure*—to their intrinsic worth. Our Saviour uses this word 'harmless'—that is, pure, sincere—in his description of what his followers should be. (Matt. 10:16.) **The sons of God.** Omit 'the,' and translate *children of God.* (Revised Version.) It is an emphatic summing up of the character expressed in the two previous words. **Without rebuke** (or, *blemish*). They are not only to be children of God, but such as are without spot or blemish. **In the midst,** etc. In direct and marked contrast with this character, which they should exhibit, Paul describes the nature of their moral environment. Compare Gal. 1:4, "this present evil world." Christians are in the midst **of a crooked and perverse nation** (or, *generation,* Revised Version). 'Nation' is not a correct translation. Of the two adjectives the second, 'perverse,' or 'distorted,' 'twisted,' is stronger than the first, which means simply 'crooked.' These words recall the characteristic descriptions of Israel in the wilderness, especially Deut. 32:5, on which the apostle's mind seems to have been dwelling throughout this exhortation. Compare also Luke 9:41. Because the world is so 'crooked' and 'perverse' Christians ought all the more earnestly to exhibit the character of true children of God, a character that is above reproach before the tribunal either of the world or of the individual conscience, and in which no blemish can be discovered even by this corrupt generation, which is always so ready to carp at God's people, and so perverse and unreasonable in all its criticism. **Among whom** refers logically back to the individuals composing the 'generation,' though it has no grammatical antecedent. See Winer, p. 141; Buttman, p 282. **Ye shine** (or, *appear*). 'Shine' would require the active voice. **As lights** (or, *luminaries,* margin of Revised Version)—in allusion, not to candles or lamps, but to the great luminaries of the heavens. **In the world** should be closely connected with the preceding noun, 'luminaries,' describing their position in the physical world, not with the verb 'appear,' referring to the Christian's position in the moral world. "Christ is light, and they are luminaries." For the world (κόσμος), without the article, see Winer, p. 123.

16. Holding forth the word of life. Their office as light givers will be fulfilled when they 'hold forth the word of life,' which is moral and spiritual light to the world. Meyer translates "possessing the word of life," and claims that while the rendering 'holding forth' is linguistically correct, it is not in harmony with the figure of luminaries. The objection, however, seems somewhat forced. The apostle's mind was probably more occupied with the real nature of their work than with the figurative representation of it just given, and so he used the word 'holding forth,' rather than some word which would more exactly continue the previous imagery. Christ is properly the word of life

17 Yea, and if I be offered upon the sacrifice and service of your faith, I joy, and rejoice with you all.
18 For the same cause also do ye joy, and rejoice with me.

17 neither labour in vain. Yea, and if I am [1] offered
upon the sacrifice and service of your faith, I joy,
18 and rejoice with you all; and in the same manner
do ye also joy, and rejoice with me.

1 Gr. *poured out as a drink-offering.*

(see 1 John 1 : 1), but the gospel is here meant, as that which reveals Christ. The expression occurs nowhere else in Paul's writings. **That I may rejoice** (rather, *for my boasting*). In 1 : 26 Paul speaks of their boasting being in him, now of his boasting being in them. Compare 2 Cor. 1 : 14. This boasting is only an indirect object which they should have in view. The primary object is, of course, the glory of God and the welfare of men. Since, however, personal appeals from one beloved affect us more sometimes than higher inducements, Paul here urges this personal consideration upon the Philippians. **In** (*against*) **the day of Christ**—laid up, as it were, against that day. **That I have not run in vain**—which will be made evident on that day by the excellent character of his Philippian converts. (1 Thess. 2 : 19, 20.) **Neither laboured in vain.** The familiar metaphor of a foot-race, appearing in the first verb 'run,' now gives place to a literal description. Paul was "in labours" often. (2 Cor. 6 : 5; 11 : 23.)

17. Yea, and if I be offered, etc. The personal reference in the last verse leads him to add an expression of his willingness to do even more for them than he has ever done. He is willing, if necessary, to become a martyr for their sakes. "This is to teach the gospel from the heart, when we are prepared with our own blood to sanction what we teach." (Calvin.) This martyrdom he conceives of under the figure of a priest slain while he is offering sacrifice. The victim upon the altar is the faith of the Philippians, which Paul, the ministering priest, is engaged in offering up to God when he is slain and his blood is poured out—a most holy and precious libation. **In**—that is, *in the act of*—**the sacrifice and service of your faith.** In speaking of himself as being "poured out" (see margin of Revised Version), there is an evident allusion to the pouring out of oblations of wine in sacrificing. According to the Jewish custom, such wine offerings were poured out at the side of the altar, but Paul in writing to converted heathens has probably in mind the heathen custom in which the wine was poured upon the victim. Whether it be a mere coincidence, or something higher, Paul has nevertheless here foreshadowed not only the fact of his subsequent martyrdom, but the manner of it—by the sword.[1] **I joy,**—even if this should be the case,—**and rejoice with you all.** Some contend for the meaning "congratulate," in the second verb. Meyer especially insists on this meaning, on the ground that he could not urge them to rejoice in ver. 18 if he had already spoken of rejoicing with them. But why not, if he realizes that the statement was a startling one? Why may he not repeat, in the form of an injunction, what he had already stated as a fact? Such martyrdom would be a cause of joy to him, but he suggests that the church also will be gainers as well as himself, for, as was well said later, "the blood of the martyrs is the seed of the church." But realizing how startling the suggestion that he rejoices with them, the apostle now adds the following injunction:

18. For the same cause also do ye joy—and at the same time remember that in so doing you are only sharing a joy I have already—**and rejoice with me.**[2]

If their faith and his blood are mingled together on the altar, their joy and his should be blended over the common sacrifice. Paul throughout this Epistle strives to impress upon his readers how light a thing he considered it to be to offer his life for the sake of the gospel.

[1] The form of the hypothesis in the Greek suggests the probability of the supposition. His death seems to him by no means a remote contingency; καὶ εἰ would suggest the latter notion. Kühner §340, 7; Winer, p. 444. The present tense (σπένδομαι) indicates the nearness of the danger. In 2 Tim. 4 : 6, where he is anticipating immediate death, he uses the same tense of this verb. The two nouns, θυσίᾳ and λειτουργίᾳ, have but a single article to show that they form a single conception. Hence, the first is the act of sacrificing (Herodotus 4, 60 : 8, 99), not the victim, and the second is added to describe the priestly service which accompanied the sacrifice. The preceding preposition signifies 'in,' if θυσίᾳ be interpreted as an action; 'upon,' if it be taken to mean victim.

[2] The pronoun (αὐτὸ) is accusative after the verb and denotes cause, not manner, as in the Revised Version.

19 But I trust in the Lord Jesus to send Timotheus shortly unto you, that I also may be of good comfort when I know your state.
20 For I have no man likeminded, who will naturally care for your state.
21 For all seek their own, not the things which are Jesus Christ's.

19 But I hope in the Lord Jesus to send Timothy
shortly unto you, that I also may be of good com-
20 fort, when I know your state. For I have no man
likeminded, who will care [1] truly for your state.
21 For they all seek their own, not the things of Jesus

1 Gr. *genuinely*.

"The death of the just is no subject for tears, but for joy. If they rejoice, we should rejoice with them. For it is misplaced for us to weep while they rejoice." (Chrysostom.)

19-24. THE APOSTLE'S PURPOSE TO SEND TIMOTHY.—The apostle declares his purpose of sending Timothy (19), whose character he most highly eulogizes (20), in contrast with his fellow-laborers (21), appealing at the same time to the knowledge which the Philippians had of him (22); and after reiterating his intention to send him (23), he expresses a hope of soon coming himself (24).

19. But (δὲ). Paul now passes to the new topic of his assistants and messengers, speaking first of Timothy. The connection with the foregoing is as follows: In ver. 17 and 18 he had spoken of the possibility of his death, which his language suggests as probable; but that conviction now, as elsewhere in this Epistle, seems to yield at once to the opposite expectation of a speedy release, or at least of such an improvement in his affairs that he can dispense with Timothy's presence and services. **I trust,** rather, *hope*. (Revised Version.) The verb in the Greek has an emphatic position in the sentence. He hopes, notwithstanding his exposure to death, to be delivered, and to be able to send Timothy whom he could not have spared in case he had been condemned to die. **In the Lord Jesus.** See above, 1:4, and below, ver. 24. These words are perfectly natural to the great apostle, who could not even hope for anything except in complete submission to the Lord's will. It was in the Lord he hoped, as in the Lord his whole life moved. **Shortly**—that is, as soon as he learns what disposition is to be made of his case (see ver. 23), which he here intimates will be very soon. **To send Timothy unto you,** etc.[1]

The purpose of this mission of Timothy was to inform Paul more fully about the condition of the Philippian Church, but with his customary delicacy he indicates his confidence in them by his expectation of comfort from Timothy's report. **That I also may be of good comfort.** The verb here used is found nowhere else in the New Testament, and rarely anywhere. The imperative is sometimes found on sepulchres in the sense of "farewell." **Also.** The Philippians will be comforted by hearing from him, and he expects *also* to be comforted by news from them.

20. The reason why he selects Timothy. **Like-minded**—that is, with Timothy, not with Paul, as many commentators explain it. He naturally compares Timothy with the rest of his assistants, and says: "I have no one like him." The other comparison seems unnatural and egotistic, though Meyer thinks the apostle could not recommend him better. **Who** (ὅστις), signifies "of such a character that," and what follows shows wherein Timothy differs so remarkably from all the rest. **Will naturally** (γνησίως)—that is, by a certain natural instinct. Demosthenes uses the same word of a genuine son in opposition to an adopted son, and uses the adverb here employed to signify an inherited and instinctive manner. Hence the apostle intimates that Timothy's interest will not be forced or feigned, but spontaneous and natural. **Care**—that is, with anxious solicitude. Our Saviour uses this word when he forbids thought of the morrow. See Matt. 6:34. Timothy must have been a more than ordinary character to have won such high praise from a man like Paul, whose regard and affection continued unabated to the end of his life.

21. In contrast with this beautiful character of Timothy the apostle describes the selfishness of the rest. **For all seek their own.** "It was a very keen sense by which Paul perceived this." (Bengel.) So severe has this censure seemed, that many have attempted to soften it by weakening the force of the words

[1] The dative (ὑμῖν) is a peculiar but not unclassical usage, implying that the mission was for their benefit; the ordinary construction would be πρὸς ὑμᾶς. See ver. 25.

22 But ye know the proof of him, that, as a son with the father, he hath served with me in the gospel.
23 Him therefore I hope to send presently, so soon as I shall see how it will go with me.
24 But I trust in the Lord that I also myself shall come shortly.

22 Christ. But ye know the proof of him, that, as a
child *serveth* a father, *so* he served with me in
23 furtherance of the gospel. Him therefore I hope to
send forthwith, so soon as I shall see how it will go
24 with me: but I trust in the Lord that I myself also

to "almost all," but this is not permissible. The only modification allowable, springs not from the language, but from a consideration of the fact, that only those available for such a mission, not the entire Roman brotherhood, can be here alluded to, and that, with the exception of Timothy, none of the apostle's well-known friends and associates appear to have been in Rome at this time. This certainly seems evident from the absence of any such greetings from individuals at the close of the Epistle as Paul was accustomed to send. It is of course impossible to tell on whom the apostle's censure rested, but probably Demas was a representative of the class. How different a picture of the apostolic church these few words give us, from that almost perfect vision which floats before our imagination, when the primitive church is mentioned! Judged by such hints as these from the writings of Paul, —the most charitable of critics,—the apostolic church was not only not the ideal church many imagine it to have been, but far inferior to the churches in modern times. How sorely Paul's heart was tried by the fickleness and worldliness of co-laborers, appears most clearly in an epistle, written at a later date, the Second to Timothy.

22. The Philippians from their own knowledge are able to substantiate Paul's good opinion of Timothy, for they **know the proof of him,** or rather his approved character. Compare 2 Cor. 2: 9; 9: 13. "Rare praise." (Bengel.) Timothy had been present at Philippi twice in Paul's company. (Acts 16: 1, 3, compared with 19: 22; 20: 4.) He may also have been there at other times, as Paul was accustomed to send him upon special embassies to the churches. See 1 Cor. 4: 17; 16: 10. At any rate, he seems to have been personally well known to the church there.

The following sentence contains the substance of their personal experience with Timothy; he had assisted Paul **as a son with a father.** In writing this thought the apostle begins as if he were about to say, as a son serves a father he has served me, but his nice sense of propriety restrains him from speaking of any one serving himself, and so he changes the construction and says, **he hath served with me.**[1]

This service had been rendered **in the gospel**—or, as in Revised Version, "in furtherance of the gospel."

23. Him therefore. The pronoun is put first with emphasis; this one, being such, I hope to send. In ver. 19, where the hope was the chief thought in his mind, we have the verb first. **So soon as I shall see.** The verb means see from a distance, hence to see forward to the end. Compare Heb. 12: 2. As soon as Paul sees clearly how it will go with him (literally, *the things concerning me*) he will send Timothy. To what special matters he alludes is uncertain, but it is evident that he was looking for some immediate change in his condition, for better or for worse. The Common Version translates the adverb *presently*, but it is rather *immediately*, or, *forthwith* (Revised Version), indicating a nearer point of time, while "shortly," in the next verse points forward to a more distant, though still near future. He will send Timothy immediately and come himself soon.

24. But I trust in the Lord that I also shall come shortly. His expectation of soon coming himself is like his hope of sending Timothy 'in the Lord.' Compare James 4: 15. We observe the same wavering and uncertainty about his future as in 1: 22, seq.; but here, as there, hope of release predominates. Compare Philem. 22, where he expresses a more assured expectation of freedom. Whether this expectation was realized or not cannot be satisfactorily determined, but the intimations of the pastoral epistles, as well as the unvarying testimony of tradition, are all in favor of the view that his hope was fulfilled.

25-30. INFORMATION CONCERNING HIS

[1] The dative is due to this first construction which was in the apostle's mind, and depends on the verb (δουλεύει) understood.

25 Yet I supposed it necessary to send to you Epaphroditus, my brother, and companion in labour, and fellow soldier, but your messenger, and he that ministered to my wants.
26 For he longed after you all, and was full of heaviness, because that ye had heard that he had been sick.
27 For indeed he was sick nigh unto death: but God

25 shall come shortly But I counted it necessary to
send to you Epaphroditus, my brother and fellow-
worker and fellow-soldier, and your [1] messenger and
26 minister to my need; since he longed [2] after you all,
and was sore troubled, because ye had heard that he
27 was sick: for indeed he was sick nigh unto death:

1 Gr. *apostle*......2 Many ancient authorities read *to see you all*.

Present Messenger, Epaphroditus. — The apostle thinks it necessary to send Epaphroditus (25), on account of that disciple's homesickness (26), who had but just recovered from an almost fatal illness (27). Hence, the apostle makes haste to send him (28), urging the Philippians, at the same time, to receive him with all joy (29), because he had risked his very life for the work of Christ (30).

25. Notwithstanding the probability that Timothy, and even he himself, will soon visit them, **I supposed[1] it necessary to send to you Epaphroditus**—that is, at present, for the reason explained in ver. 26-28. He was very likely a resident of Philippi (there is no reason to identify him with the Epaphras of Col. 1 : 7; 4 : 12, who was a Colossian Christian), and is supposed by some to have been the pastor of the church. Paul evinces his high regard for him by the manner in which he refers to him. He calls him his brother, fellow-worker, and fellow-soldier, in which description we observe a climax; he shares the same relationship, toils, dangers; he is also the Philippians' 'messenger' and 'minister' to the apostle. The first of these last two epithets is used in its etymological significance, "one sent." Compare 2 Cor. 8 : 23. There is no allusion to his "apostleship" in any sense. He is also the 'minister' to the apostle's needs by bringing a contribution from the Philippians to him. See 4 : 18. The simple verb in the Greek "to send" is used in the sense of the compound to send back, a common usage. If, however, as Bengel conjectures, Epaphroditus had been sent to stay with the apostle, the simple form would be the more appropriate; as his companion, he simply sends him.

26. The reason for his sending Epaphroditus was chiefly his homesickness. **For he longed**—*is longing*. Epistolary imperfect. See on ver. 25.[2] In this longing "something of nature may have been mingled, but when grace prevails all things are estimated by love." (Bengel.) **And was** (*is*) **full of heaviness.** Suidas defines this verb as signifying "to be exceedingly sorrowful." Others make the meaning to be "foreign" (from α and δῆμος), and hence "homeless," "wretched." In either case it is a strong word, expressive of great distress of mind, and is used by Matthew to describe our Lord's agony in the garden. (Matt. 26 : 37.) **Because that ye had** (or, *have*) **heard.** In some way unknown to us, Epaphroditus had heard that the news of his sickness had reached Philippi, and probably, also, that the Philippians were much distressed about him; and this information had produced a deep feeling of homesickness, a feeling so intense that the apostle describes it as a condition of mental wretchedness. In the very words of this description we realize the tenderness of the apostle's sympathy with the homesick disciple.

27. The report the Philippians had received was true, **for[3] indeed he was sick.** The sickness had been well nigh fatal, but God had restored him, showing mercy not to him alone, but to Paul also, whose heart would

[1] The tense of the principal verb in this and ver. 26 and 28 is aorist, but probably refers to the very time when Paul was writing, and, therefore, according to English usage, should be translated as present. In letters, the Greek custom was to assume the standpoint of the receiver, and to put the writer's present thoughts and purposes into a past tense. We should, however, say, "I think it necessary," "he is longing after you all and is full of heaviness," etc. See Winer, p. 278; Goodwin's "Greek Moods and Tenses," § 17, note 5. The tenses in these verses we suppose to be epistolary aorist and imperfect, in accordance with the very probable conjecture that Epaphroditus was the bearer of this Epistle.

[2] The Greek participle and the copula are more expressive than the finite verb, just as "is longing" in English pictures the condition better than the simple "longs." See Winer, p. 348.

[3] The words καὶ γὰρ express a strong confirmation: they imply a suppressed thought: and (the information received was true) for, etc. See Hadley's "Greek Grammar," 870 a. d.

had mercy on him; and not on him only, but on me also, lest I should have sorrow upon sorrow.

28 I sent him therefore the more carefully, that, when ye see him again, ye may rejoice, and that I may be the less sorrowful.

29 Receive him therefore in the Lord with all gladness; and hold such in reputation:

30 Because for the work of Christ he was nigh unto death, not regarding his life, to supply your lack of service toward me.

but God had mercy on him; and not on him only,
but on me also, that I might not have sorrow upon
28 sorrow. I have sent him therefore the more dili-
gently, that, when ye see him again, ye may re-
29 joice, and that I may be the less sorrowful. Receive
him therefore in the Lord with all joy: and hold such
30 in honour; because for the work of [1] Christ he came
nigh unto death, hazarding his life to supply that
which was lacking in your service toward me.

1 Many ancient authorities read *the Lord*.

have been weighed down by **sorrow upon sorrow** had he been taken away. To the sorrow of his own imprisonment and sufferings would have been added the greater sorrow of the loss of his dear friend. How beautifully the apostle describes the blessing of Epaphroditus's recovery as God's mercy to himself! "He does not boast of stoical apathy, as if he had been insensible and exempt from human affections." (Calvin.) This whole passage shows that the apostolic gift of miraculous power was not one to be used at any time. Such power was "the sign of an apostle" (2 Cor. 12: 12), and was probably only used as an attestation of their divine mission. Some divine intimation was undoubtedly given when its use was permitted. In all other cases, the apostles were relegated to the same resource as other Christians; namely, the throne of God, where they could bring their burdens and cast them on the Lord (Ps. 55: 22) in prayer, and hope for the same sustaining grace that is granted to all believers.

28. I sent (*send*)—epistolary aorist. See on ver. 25. **Therefore**—on account of his state of mind. **The more carefully**—rather, *speedily;* that is, than I should otherwise have done. See Winer, p. 213. In the last part of this verse we have another exquisite phrase, flowing right from the apostle's heart, **that ye may rejoice, and I be the less sorrowful.** Paul could not use the word 'rejoice' of himself in these circumstances, for his heart was naturally sad at parting with his companion, but he would at least be less sorrowful, as he thought of the joy of the greeting in Philippi between these beloved friends.[1]

29. Receive him therefore—that is, in accordance with my purpose in sending him, of making you glad. As Paul has intended to increase their joy, they should welcome him **with all gladness** (*joy*), and also **in the Lord**—that is, with a truly Christian greeting (compare Rom. 16: 2); **and hold such in reputation**—or, *honor*. The apostle glances aside at the whole brotherhood of Christian workers, and bespeaks for them the regard of the Philippians; at the same time, his wider reference is but the glance of his eye, as it were; for he continues in the next verse to speak of the great merits of Epaphroditus and his high deserts.

30. The sickness of Epaphroditus had been incurred in the way of duty. Paul does not tell us definitely either the cause or character of this sickness; he simply informs us that it was contracted while engaged in the Lord's service. It seems most probable that he had brought it upon himself on the journey to Rome by his anxious desire to reach the apostle rather than by his attendance upon the apostle in his imprisonment. It hardly comports with what we know of Paul's generous regard for the health and comfort of others to suppose that he would suffer Epaphroditus to receive an injury by over-exertion in attendance upon himself. **Not regarding his life.** The exact reading of the original is here uncertain. The manuscripts give us two words, both of them peculiar: "lightly regarding" (παραβουλευσάμενος), and "staking," "hazarding" (παραβολευσάμενος). As the former has the more familiar sound, being a compound of a common verb, it is more likely to have been substituted for the latter by some copyist than the reverse. Besides, the latter is better attested, being found in the best manuscripts.[2]

[1] In accordance with Paul's rule of placing πάλιν either before the verb or immediately after it, the translation should be "that when ye see him, ye may rejoice again," rather than as in the Common and the Revised Versions, "when ye see him again," etc.

[2] The verb from which this participle comes occurs nowhere else, but is evidently derived from παράβολος "staking," "risking," and means "to stake," "to hazard," just as περπερεύεσθαι from πέρπερος, "boasting," "bragging," means "to boast," "to brag."

CHAPTER III.

FINALLY, my brethren, rejoice in the Lord. To write the same things to you, to me indeed *is* not grevious, but for you *it is* safe.

1 Finally, my brethren, [1] rejoice in the Lord. To write the same things to you, to me indeed is not

1 Or, *farewell.*

Epaphroditus is represented as staking his life as a gambler stakes his money. In using this word Paul did not probably intend to convey any reproach, but only to mark his utter intrepidity and unselfishness. He had, with an almost recklessness of holy zeal, risked his very life for the work of Christ, and the prominent mention of this purpose of his devotion relieves the apostle's language of any appearance of the censure that might lie in the word he uses. In after times certain brotherhoods, who nursed the sick and buried the dead, were called *parabolani*, a name doubtless derived from this very passage. **To supply your lack of service toward me.** The apostle has told us that Epaphroditus fell sick while engaged in the work of Christ, and now he defines more particularly the special task on which he was bent—that is, supplying the Philippians' lack of service toward himself. The original does not contain the slight tinge of reproach to the church which the English version seems to convey, but suggests rather a graceful compliment both to Epaphroditus and to the Philippians. Epaphroditus, he says, sought to supply the lack of you in the service rendered me.[1] Luther's version well expresses the sense: "that he might serve me in your stead." How delicately he suggests that the absence of the Philippians was a sort of flaw in the gift, which their presence would have made perfect, but which their messenger exerted himself most zealously to supply. With such zeal and even recklessness did he enter into the spirit of the church in their heartfelt contribution, that he exposed his life to utmost danger, and by this noble unselfishness made up, as it were, for the lack of the personal ministrations of the Philippians in bringing and presenting their gift. The compound verb is appropriately and even elegantly chosen, as it hints that the vacuum was only partial, while the simple verb would have suggested an entire vacuum. Epaphroditus filled up this partial lack, until the whole transaction was complete. Erasmus well defines the meaning of the compound verb as "to fill by addition what was lacking to perfect fullness." Compare 1 Cor. 16 : 17; 2 Cor. 11 : 9; Gal. 6 : 2; Col. 1 : 24. Menken well says of the mission of Epaphroditus: "It was not a trifling act for a Christian, one of a sect everywhere spoken against, everywhere hated and oppressed, which found no protection under Jewish or Gentile rule, to travel from Philippi to Rome, in order to carry aid to a Christian teacher, an apostle, yea, the hated and now imprisoned Paul, over whose approaching death his enemies were already rejoicing, and take his stand publicly before the world, by the side of this man, and say, 'I am his friend."

Ch. 3 : 1-16. WARNING AGAINST FALSE TEACHERS ENFORCED BY A REFERENCE TO HIS OWN EXAMPLE.—Apparently about to bring his Epistle to a close (1), Paul is led, by some unknown occasion of thought or suggestion, to utter an indignant warning against false teachers (2), which serves to introduce the contrast of his own example (3). After a rapid sketch of his superior claims from a Judaistic and legal point of view (4-6), he declares his utter renunciation of all such claims (7, 8), and his entire reliance on Christ (9, 10), together with his humble striving after perfection (12-14), and urges his readers to imitate his example and to walk in unity (16).

1. Finally. In Paul's writings this word generally indicates the near close of an Epistle, and serves to introduce an additional exhortation, warning, encouragement, etc. See ch. 4 : 8; Eph. 6 : 10; 2 Cor. 13 : 11; 2 Thess. 3 : 1. Sometimes the concluding portion is considerably prolonged, as in **First Thessalonians**, where it occupies two chapters. The use of this word would seem to indicate that Paul was about to bring his letter to a close,

[1] According to the interpretation given above, the personal pronoun ὑμῶν belongs only to the noun ὑστέρημα, "lack of you," while the following genitive denotes in what respect: "in respect to the service rendered me." See Winer, p. 191.

2 Beware of dogs, beware of evil workers, beware of the concision.

2 irksome, but for you it is safe. Beware of the dogs, beware of the evil workers, beware of the concision;

and the remarks about Timothy and Epaphroditus in the last chapter point in the same direction, for it was Paul's custom to refer to his fellow-laborers at the end of his Epistles; but the abrupt change of tone in ver. 2 suggests that he was diverted from that purpose. The mere length of the concluding portion would not necessarily indicate a change of plan, but the difference of manner is so great, with no ostensible cause for it, as to lead us to adopt the explanation that he met with some kind of interruption, after which he took up an entirely new train of thought. It would appear as if the apostle when he wrote 'finally' was about to utter those general exhortations and concluding messages which occupy 4 : 4-23, since he begins with the injunction 'rejoice,' found in 4 : 4, and all between seems like a lengthy digression. **Rejoice.** This joy is to be **in the Lord,** not the joy of worldlings, but "spiritual gladness." (Theodoret.) How constantly this suggestive phrase drops from the pen of the apostle! 'In the Lord' his whole life and thought moved, as in their proper sphere. Joy in the Lord is one of the fruits of the Spirit. (Gal. 6 : 22; compare Rom. 14 : 17; 1 Thess. 1 : 6.) **To write the same things.** Much controversy has arisen over the exact reference of these words, and a perfectly satisfactory decision seems unattainable. The simplest solution is to refer them to the preceding words, 'rejoice in the Lord,' but why should he say, **for you it is safe,** to have such an injunction continually repeated? That word 'safe' evidently implies a reference to warning rather than encouraging words. Besides, the exhortation is not repeated, for it has not appeared before in this Epistle. If then we refer this apology to the following words, in what way are they repeated? They also have not appeared before in this Epistle. They must then have occurred in his oral instructions, in his communications by means of messengers, or in some other letter. But in the first two cases he would not have said 'to write the same things,' for he had not written them before; but he would either have used some word including both oral and written forms of communication, as "to repeat, to advise," or in some other way have suggested such a reference. Certainly the words, as they stand, indicate that he had *written* these things before somewhere, and hence we are driven to the supposition of some written communication to the Philippians, no longer in existence. There seems in the minds of many a strong aversion against believing that any written words of an apostle could have been lost; but what of the letter to the Laodiceans? Is it hard to believe that Paul wrote more than once to a church so well beloved, as that at Philippi, which had again and again contributed to his necessities? To set this conclusion almost beyond doubt, we have in the Epistle of Polycarp to the Philippians a reference to the letters (plural) which the Apostle Paul wrote them. (3 : 2, and Zahn's Note.) Admitting then the reference to such a previous written communication, we must suppose that Paul had therein warned the Philippians against false teachers. Something now calls his attention at this point to the insidious efforts of those false teachers to corrupt his disciples and destroy his teachings, and he bursts out into a vehement warning against them, prefixing first as an apology the statement that he is willing to write, and they need to hear the same things. "Men are dull to conceive, hard to believe, apt to forget, slow to practice heavenly truths, and had therefore great need to have them much pressed and often inculcated." (Trapp.) With this interpretation we must suppose a longer or shorter pause between the two sentences in this verse, after which the apostle proceeds in an entirely different strain. Another notable example of such an entire change of manner is found in the concluding portion of Second Corinthians, commencing at chapter 10.

2. The abruptness with which these warnings are introduced and their peculiar form, gives plausibility to Meyer's view, that they are couched in the very same words previously employed. **Beware!**[1]—rather, *behold.* Compare Mark 4 : 24; 1 Cor. 1 : 26; 10 : 18; 2 John 8. This meaning, however, involves the other:

[1] 'Beware' would require the preposition ἀπό after the verb. See Mark 8 : 15; 12 : 38.

"see and you will beware." (Bengel.) It is thrice repeated in the intensity of his feeling, "like three peals of a trumpet." **Of** (*the*[1]) **dogs.** (Revised Version.)

Some commentators have tried to distinguish three classes of opponents in this threefold description, but we are rather to see three different designations of the same hostile party, describing them according to their character, activity, and creed. They are "Jews, who preach at the same time both Christianity and Judaism, corrupting the gospel." (Chrysostom.) First, we have their character indicated by the contemptuous term 'dogs.' The dog is not the friend and companion of man in the Orient, as he is among Western nations. There he is an object of utter contempt. He roams the streets, without a home or master, lives on vile refuse, quarrels with other curs, and snaps viciously at every passer-by. Hence in all Oriental literature and language 'dog' is a most opprobious epithet. The Mohammedans at this day apply it to Christians; the ancient Jews applied it to all Gentiles; while the Greek also used the word contemptuously, though not applying it to any special nation or religion. A hint of an occasionally different and higher view of the dog is afforded in the story of Ulysses' dog Argos. (Odyssey 17, 290, seq. Compare also Æschylus "Agamemnon" 590.) By the term 'dog' the Jews meant to suggest the idea of impurity, and hence applied it to all foreigners, who were at least ceremonially impure and profane. (Deut. 23:18; Matt. 15:26.) In the mouth of a Greek the word symbolized "impudence." Paul now retorts upon these Jewish teachers the very word of reproach they were accustomed to hurl at the Gentiles. "They are now called dogs, who are unwilling to be the Israel of God." (Bengel.) To the foregoing figurative description of their character, he now adds a literal description of their activity. **Evil workers.** Compare 2 Cor. 11 : 13. The well-known Jewish zeal and activity (Rom. 10:2) characterized this dangerous party in the Christian Church, and the results of this activity were as bad as that of the Pharisees, who compassed sea and land to make one proselyte; and made him twofold more a son of hell than themselves. (Matt. 23:15.) They were 'evil workers,' for they were working against God. "They work, but for a bad end, and a work that is much worse than idleness, for they tear up the foundations that have been well laid." (Chrysostom.) Lastly, he styles them **the concision,** in contemptuous allusion to their peculiar pride and boast. They boasted of their circumcision, but Paul would not allow them this noble term, and so by a sarcastic paranomasia he describes them as the concision, the mutilation. ("curti Judaei," "Hor. Sat." 1, 9, 70.) The corresponding verb is used by the Septuagint to describe such cuttings and mutilations as were forbidden by the Mosaic law. (Lev. 21:5; 1 Kings 18:28.) Hence Paul would indicate by the use of this term, that the circumcision in which they gloried was, after all, nothing but a mutilation of the body, such as the heathen delighted in. "They did nothing but to cut their flesh." (Chrysostom.) There was nothing more to it, no spiritual significance, such as always was the case with true circumcision, even under the Old Covenant. (Deut. 10:16; 30:6; Jer. 4:4; Rom. 2:28, 29.) Paul speaks in this contemptuous way of circumcision, because in the case of these false teachers it had lost all spiritual significance and worth; at the same time he never combats the observance of the rite among born Jews (1 Cor. 7:18, 19), but only the thrusting of it upon the Gentiles (Gal. 5:1, 2), contrary to the spirit of the gospel. In the case of Timothy, Paul himself performed the rite, in order to give him a greater influence over the Jews (Acts 16:3); but he resolutely refused to allow Titus, a Gentile, to be circumcised (Gal. 2:3-5), and in this he was supported by the other apostles, who in the celebrated conference at Jerusalem drew up a sort of programme for the Gentile churches, in which circumcision is not even mentioned. (Acts 15:23-29.) For a still more sarcastic allusion to circumcision, see Gal. 5 : 12. Such plays on words are common to all languages. Meyer refers to Luther's tendency in this direction. They are more frequent in Paul's writings than elsewhere in the New Testament. (See Winer, p. 636.)

The party here referred to cannot be those mentioned in 1 : 15, because he does not speak of a danger threatening the church in Rome, but of a danger menacing the Philippians

[1] The article indicates a well-known class.

3 For we are the circumcision, which worship God in the spirit, and rejoice in Christ Jesus, and have no confidence in the flesh.
4 Though I might also have confidence in the flesh. If any other man thinketh that he hath whereof he might trust in the flesh, I more:

3 for we are the circumcision, who worship by the Spirit of God, and glory in Christ Jesus, and have
4 no confidence in the flesh; though I myself might have confidence even in the flesh: if any other man [1]thinketh to have confidence in the flesh, I

[1] Or, seemeth.

themselves; nor of a peculiar phase of Christian teaching, but of anti-Christian teaching, whose aim was to lead the Gentile Christians over to Judaism. It was undoubtedly the same party against which he inveighs so vehemently in the letter to the Galatians, only here they had not yet found a foothold as in Galatia, because had that been the case, Paul would surely have blamed the Philippians, as he did the Galatians; but he does not allude to a single trace of doctrinal impurity in the former church. The danger in their case was a threatening danger. Whether the Jewish party had yet appeared there, is uncertain, but it is evident that Paul apprehended its immediate advent, if it was not already present. When it is remembered that the violent antagonism of the Jews drove him out of the neighboring city of Thessalonica, on his first appearance there, and even pursued him to the city of Berea, and drove him away from there also (Acts 17:5-14), it will not seem at all strange that Paul should have felt called upon to warn the Philippians most earnestly against this insidious Jewish activity.

3. He now proceeds to show why he has characterized those Judaizers as 'the concision,' by describing the true circumcision. **For we,** emphatic by position; not they, but we—whether circumcised in the flesh or not—who are described in the following words: "If you must seek circumcision, he says, you will find it among us who worship God in spirit." (Chrysostom.) Since Christ has come who is "the end of the law for righteousness" (Rom. 10:4), and has abrogated the old circumcision with all the rest of the ceremonial law (Col. 3:11), the only genuine circumcision is that of the heart. (Col. 2:11.) "Bodily circumcision was now useless, nay hurtful." (Bengel.) In the three following clauses, which form an anti-climax, the features of the truly circumcised are delineated. **Which worship God in the Spirit**—or, *by the Spirit of God.* (Revised Version.) This rendering, though an unusual form of expression, is founded upon a better reading in the Greek than that on which the Common Version is based. The verb (λατρεύοντες) is the ordinary, and almost technical one for describing the peculiar worship of Israel (Luke 2:37; Acts 26:7; Heb. 9:9; 10:2; Rom. 9:4), and so quietly suggests, that the true form of worship, which was once characteristic of the Jewish people alone, has been transferred to the Christian Church. According to Paul, Christianity is the true successor of Judaism; Christians possess the true circumcision, and offer the true worship. Assisted by the Holy Ghost, who "helpeth our infirmities" (Rom. 8:26), Christians are enabled to offer that worship which the Father seeks, a worship unfettered by forms or places; which may be presented anywhere and at any time, for which the open field is a sanctuary as well as temple or church, and whose chief features are spirituality and truth. (John 4:23, 24; Rom. 8.) **And rejoice** (*glory*) **in Christ Jesus**—not in anything outward, in distinctions and badges and "carnal ordinances, imposed until the time of reformation" (Heb. 9:10), or in works of righteousness (Gal. 2:16), but in him who is the fountain of our spiritual life. (Gal. 6:14.) Compare Jer. 9:23, 24. Having in Christ all that was typified in the rites and ceremonies of the Old Covenant, possessing in him the substance itself, they could not, like those Judaizers, esteem so highly the ancient and venerable, but already vanishing shadows of things to come. Even the very privileges of the Abrahamic covenant itself were theirs. (Gal. 3:14.) As the spiritual had now become the only ground of distinction, the true Israel of God **have no confidence in the flesh,** either in circumcision, or in any of the rites, ceremonies, and privileges connected with it. Those false teachers reposed their whole trust in the flesh, and taught others to do the same (Gal. 6:13); but the true people of God abjure all such confidence.

4. Though I (*myself*) **might also have confidence in the flesh.** He singles himself out as offering an exception, in certain respects, to those described above. That exception consists in his ability to boast of Jewish

5 Circumcised the eighth day, of the stock of Israel, of the tribe of Benjamin, a Hebrew of the Hebrews; as touching the law, a Pharisee;

5 yet more: circumcised the eighth day, of the stock of Israel, of the tribe of Benjamin, a Hebrew of

prerogatives, if they were of any worth. Paul seeks, in the following enumeration of his special claims, to prove that his hostility to Judaistic teaching does not spring from envy. If he had been a Gentile, or even if as a Jew he had possessed only inferior claims, his opposition might with more reason be credited to jealousy; but the fact was that none could boast of higher Jewish claims than he, and few could even equal him. In 2 Cor. 11 : 18, seq., there is a striking resemblance to this passage, both in substance and tone, although the former is a still more hot and indignant arraignment of his adversaries, "The first belongs to the crisis of the struggle, the other to its close." In Rom. 11 : 1 there is a still briefer appeal to his Jewish claims. The words of the previous clause 'having no confidence in the flesh' seem to have started the apostle on this line of self-defense. This "going off at a word," as it is expressively described by Paley, is especially characteristic of Paul's writings. ("Horae Paulinæ," vi., 3.) 'Might also have,' etc. Neither the Common nor the Revised Version exactly reproduces the thought. The apostle does not say he 'might have,' but 'has.' The Greek, literally, is "though I, having confidence also in the flesh." He actually possesses all these claims, but renounces them as of no worth.[1] "Having, not using." (Bengel.) For the moment, Paul proceeds to state these claims as if they were something real. He uses an *argumentum ad hominem*, assumes the standpoint of his adversaries, and overthrows them with their own weapons. If one who had such superior Jewish claims could count them worthless, what must be said of the folly of those Judaizers who extol so highly their own inferior merits? **If any man thinketh**—that is, *supposeth* (Matt. 3 : 9)—**that he hath whereof he might trust.** All these words are the translation of but a single word in the Greek, meaning "to trust" (πεποιθέναι). The apostle simply says, "if any other supposeth he can trust in the flesh, I more," for the reasons given below, especially ver. 6.

5. He describes first his hereditary privileges, and then his personal religious characteristics. Compare 2 Cor. 11 : 22, seq. The several points are enumerated very briefly "on the fingers, as it were." (Bengel.) **Circumcised the eighth day.** He was then neither an Ishmaelite, who would have been circumcised at the age of thirteen, nor a proselyte, who would have received circumcision in mature life. In his case, the sacred rite, of which the Jews were always so proud, had been received in its perfection. (Gen. 17 : 12; Lev. 12 : 3.) **Of the stock of Israel.** Paul might have been the son of a proselyte, who, though he had not received the rite of circumcision in its perfection himself, desired to bestow that privilege upon his son, and had circumcised him the eighth day; and hence he says, in opposition to any such state of the case, that he was of Israelitish stock; that is, his parents were also of the privileged race. **Of the tribe of Benjamin**—of that tribe which alone had stood by the side of Judah in steadfast loyalty to the throne of David and to the worship of Jehovah, and on whose soil stood the Holy City and the temple. **A Hebrew of the Hebrews** completes the notion of his purity of lineage, by stating that his ancestors were all of the Hebrew race from time immemorial. There had been no admixture of Gentile blood in any of the past generations. If, as has been conjectured from this language, his opponents were not of pure Jewish extraction, these features of Paul's hereditary claims must have given a terrible blow to their haughty pretensions and justified his claim of superiority from a Jewish standpoint. It is, however, in the following claims, perhaps, that we may discover the special reason of his statement that if any one presumes to trust in the flesh, he more. As an adherent of the Ancient Covenant, he had lived a most exemplary religious life. First of all, **as touching the law, a Pharisee**—a member of the "straitest sect" among the Jews. Compare Acts 26 : 5. They were noted for their devotion to the law, and were the orthodox

[1] Had Paul used the participle of the previous clause (πεποιθώς) he would have represented himself as actually putting confidence in the flesh, and so he varies the expression and says (ἔχων πεποίθησιν), "having a confidence," which he might use, and once did most highly esteem, but now renounces.

6 Concerning zeal, persecuting the church; touching the righteousness which is in the law, blameless.
7 But what things were gain to me, those I counted loss for Christ.
8 Yea doubtless, and I count all things but loss for the excellency of the knowledge of Christ Jesus my Lord: for whom I have suffered the loss of all things, and do count them *but* dung, that I may win Christ,

6 Hebrews; as touching the law, a Pharisee; as touching zeal, persecuting the church; as touching the righteousness which is in the law, found blameless.
7 Howbeit what things were [1]gain to me, these
8 have I counted loss for Christ. Yea verily, and I count all things to be loss for the excellency of the knowledge of Christ Jesus my Lord: for whom I suffered the loss of all things, and do count them

1 Gr. *gains*.

party in the nation. See Josephus "Life," 38; "Wars of the Jews," ii., 8, 14. The apostle was not only a Pharisee himself, but the son of Pharisees; that is, he had a Pharisaic ancestry for generations perhaps (Acts 23 : 6; see Meyer's note), and had been educated in Jerusalem in the most famous school of that sect, "at the feet of Gamaliel." (Acts 22 : 3.)

6. As a Pharisee his zeal had been exhibited in a most convincing way. **Concerning zeal, persecuting the church.** This he speaks of in the present tense, as if that dreadful service, of which he had so bitterly repented (1 Cor. 15 : 9; 1 Tim. 1 : 13), were still a present claim upon Jewish regard, as indeed it would be, if he had remained a Jew. If, then, any could claim high distinction in Jewish estimation, he, as a persecutor of the church, could equal any and surpass most of his Pharisaic rivals. Finally, he says, **touching the righteousness which is in the law,**—that is, consists in obedience to the mere letter,—**blameless**—of course, only from a legal standpoint; and Paul gives a very different account of himself from the higher Christian standpoint. See Rom. 7. "There is a twofold righteousness of the law. The one of these is spiritual, consisting in the perfect love of God and of our neighbors; this is contained in the doctrinal statement, but was never actually found in the life of any individual. The other is righteousness according to the letter, and may appear in the sight of men." (Calvin.) From the standpoint of his opponents, what more could be said in any one's favor? His hereditary claims were superior to those of most Jews, while his conduct left nothing to be desired. He was a Pharisee, a zealous Pharisee, a blameless Pharisee. In his adherence to the law, his zeal for the law, observance of the law, few could equal, none surpass him.

7. All these things had been an advantage to him as a Jew, and so he says: **What things were gain to me**—not *supposed* gain, but *real* gain. They had given him reputation among the people, laid the foundation of his hopes and aspirations, and, above all, satisfied his conscience, in the days when the spiritual nature of God's demands was not yet revealed to him. But now all these advantages were of no value in his sight. **Those I counted loss for Christ.** The Revised Version translates "have I counted loss." The perfect tense suggests the idea that he began at the time of his conversion, and has continued to the present moment to estimate them so. Observe the significance of the change from the plural "gains," as in the margin of the Revised Version, to the singular 'loss.' The plural suggests the various elements of gain which had grown up out of those high claims, while the singular hints that he lumps them all together as a single item of loss. The things he had once so painstakingly reckoned up one by one as gains, he now dismisses at once with a single word, 'loss.' "When he spoke of 'gain,' he said, 'they were gain.' But when he spoke of loss, 'I counted.' And this rightly; for the former was naturally so, but the latter became so 'from my opinion.'" (Chrysostom.) 'For Christ.' Below, ver. 8-11, he explains more fully why he counts them loss for Christ's sake. If he was going to possess Christ, he must renounce all other claims, which would be nothing but a hindrance to his perfect trust in him. See Gal. 5 : 2-4. He must part with all other treasures for the sake of this one "pearl of great price." (Matt. 13 : 45, 46.) "Paul is content to part with a sky full of stars for one Sun of righteousness." (Trapp.) "Seest thou, how everywhere he calls it loss, not absolutely, but for Christ. . . . When the sun shines it is loss to sit in candle light." (Chrysostom.)

8. He unfolds still farther the statement of ver. 7, emphasizing and amplifying it. **Yea doubtless, and I count all things but loss.** The emphasis is on the words 'all things,' which extend the scope of his previous statement, making it embrace every conceiv-

9 And be found in him, not having mine own righteousness, which is of the law, but that which is through the faith of Christ, the righteousness which is of God by faith:

9 but refuse, that I may gain Christ, and be found in him, [1] not having a righteousness of my own, *even* that which is of the law, but that which is through faith in Christ, the righteousness which is

1 Or, *not having as my righteousness that which is of the law.*

able claim and merit from a human standpoint. Whatever he might once have counted gain, he now counts but loss. **For the excellency of the knowledge**—because this knowledge surpasses everything else in value. **Of Christ Jesus**—who has now become the greatest gain of his life. In the glow of heartfelt gratitude he adds the words **my Lord.** This clause begins the unfolding of the meaning of the words 'for Christ' in the previous verse. There he simply said 'for Christ,' here he expands those words into 'for the excellency of the knowledge of Christ Jesus,' and below, ver. 10, he develops the special features of this knowledge. **For whom I have suffered the loss of all things.** Paul has not only counted all things loss, but has actually suffered the loss of all things.[1] And yet he does not regret it, for intensifying his previous expression he says, **and do count them but dung** (or, *refuse*, the Revised Version). The word translated dung is a common one in the Greek, and its general meaning well established; but its exact etymology is uncertain, some deriving it from a phrase signifying "to throw to the dogs," others from a word meaning dung. It signifies all kinds of refuse, rubbish, sweepings, husks, dung, etc. Thus intensely did Paul repudiate all those things he once set so much store by; he counted them as mere 'refuse,' rubbish, as something not only to be lightly esteemed, but also to be utterly cast out of his heart, just as dung is with loathing swept out of doors. "Since it is likely they would say that the righteousness which comes from toil is the greater, he shows that it is dung in comparison with the other." (Chrysostom.) "Paul's sublime spirit counts all dung, yet is content, for Christ, to be counted the offscouring of all things." (Trapp.) **That I may win Christ.** He already has Christ, but he wishes to possess him more richly. The word 'win' is peculiar, suggested by the words "loss" and "gain," on which he has been ringing so many changes. By winning Christ he means becoming so united to him that he can say, "He is mine," having him as his life, drawing nourishment from him as the branch from the vine, possessing him as his "righteousness, wisdom, sanctification, and redemption," as everything the believer desires and needs. Since it is impossible to win Christ in this way and still to hold on to those Jewish claims, he renounces them all, and renounces them gladly—yea, with something of loathing.

9. In this and the following verses we have a brief but noble description of true righteousness. **And be found in him**—the result of his winning Christ. His own unworthy self will no longer appear, but will be swallowed up, as it were, in Christ, who has taken his place before the tribunal of divine justice. God no longer looks at the sinner who has won Christ, but sees only Christ and his righteousness. That this is the thought appears from the following words: **not having mine own righteousness**—not possessing any righteousness that I might claim as my own (Rom. 10:3), such, for instance, as he once boasted of when a Pharisee, a righteousness **which is of the law**—that is, flows from obedience to the law; **but that which is through the faith of** (or, *in*) **Christ**—that righteousness which God bestows, and which is appropriated by faith.[2] God's righteousness is opposed to my righteousness, faith to law, and 'through faith' and 'upon faith' (see note below) to 'from law.' Legal righteousness looks to the law to justify, and hence it is a righteousness of the law, elsewhere described also as "by works." Christian righteousness, on the contrary, depends on faith, not, however, as a source of justification—for God alone is this—but as a means and as a condition, for faith is both the appropriating medium and the essen-

[1] The article before 'all things' in the Greek (τὰ πάντα) points out the things already mentioned or suggested, "my all," as we sometimes say in English.

[2] The various Greek prepositions are used with the nicest discrimination. The legal righteousness is described as 'of the law,' flowing from the law as its source; Christian righteousness as 'of God,' its source, 'through faith,' the medium of its appropriation, and finally 'upon faith' (see margin of Revised Version) its basis or condition.

10 That I may know him, and the power of his resurrection, and the fellowship of his sufferings, being made conformable unto his death;	10 from God [2] by faith: that I may know him, and the power of his resurrection, and the fellowship of his sufferings, becoming conformed unto his death;

2 Gr. *upon.*

tial condition of true righteousness. It may be looked at in both these lights, and Paul combines the two 'through faith' and 'upon faith' for the sake of imparting that fullness which he delights to give to such definitions. And finally this faith is described as 'of Christ' or 'in Christ,' because faith rests upon Christ and his work as its proper object. It will be seen that Paul has here given us a most comprehensive description of the righteousness of faith, both in its negative and positive aspects.

10. As the preceding verse had unfolded this new experience of Paul on the side of righteousness, so this verse unfolds it on the side of knowledge, and thus amplifies the phrase 'for the excellency of the knowledge of Christ.' **That I may know him**—not in any merely intellectual or speculative way, but by an experimental and saving knowledge, such knowledge as only comes from union with Christ—"being found in him." Union with Christ brings to the soul a knowledge such as Paul had, when he exclaimed: "I know him whom I have believed" (2 Tim. 1:12)—a knowledge that ever grows richer and deeper. "She that touched the tassel of his robe had a knowledge of Christ deeper and truer than the crowds that thronged about him; for 'virtue' had come out of him, and she felt it in herself." Two features of this knowledge, which were especially important in Paul's estimation, are now dwelt upon. First, the knowledge of **the power of his resurrection**—not simply the knowledge of his resurrection. The latter an unbeliever might have, for he might accept the resurrection as an historical fact, but the power of his resurrection only the believer can know. This power which the resurrection exerts over the Christian is not to be understood in any limited sense, but in all its fullness. The resurrection of Christ was the divine seal set upon Christ's authority (Rom. 1:4), the pledge of our redemption (Rom. 4:24, 25; 5:10; 8:34; 1 Cor. 15:17), and the prophecy of our future resurrection (Rom. 8:11); and thereby has become a most quickening and vital power in our lives. (Rom. 6:4; 1 Cor. 6:14, seq.; Eph. 2:5, 6; Col. 3:1, seq.) This wondrous power of the resurrection Paul wished to know and feel more and more. The second element of this knowledge was **the fellowship of his sufferings**—that is, to realize in all his own sufferings that he was walking in the footsteps of his Lord. He did not desire to know Christ's sufferings; that is, to suffer in the same way—that could not be—but the fellowship of them, the sense of fellowship with Christ in his trials; so that as the "Captain of our salvation" was "made perfect through suffering," he the disciple might also be; and as the sufferings of Christ were the salvation of the church, so he might, in a sense, share in that work by filling up the sufferings that remain. (Col. 1:24.) Compare 2 Cor. 1:5; Matt. 15:23. "Oh, how great is the dignity of suffering!" (Chrysostom.) Compare 1:29; 2:17. The knowledge of the fellowship of Christ's sufferings depends on the previous knowledge of the power of his resurrection, for it is this latter that gives assurance of a future life, and it is only the hope of a future life that can give any glory or meaning to suffering. It is the mighty evidential power of our Lord's resurrection that maintains our faith in the future life strong and unwavering. Except for that, we should only guess and hope, or doubt and despair. Now, without this strong unquestioning faith in the future life, we cannot know the fellowship of Christ's sufferings, for the very essence of such fellowship is the conviction that God has put us into the furnace of affliction, as he did the Master, to prepare us for his glory. Hence it is that Paul presents these two elements of knowledge in this order, which is the order of experience. "To suffer together creates a purer fellow-feeling than to labor together." "Companionship in sorrow forms the most enduring of all ties." **Being made conformable unto his death.** See also Revised Version. This is a description of the apostle's actual, present experience: "I die daily" (1 Cor. 15:31), and before long I expect to meet a martyr's fate. The phrase therefore describes the imminent peril of that

11 If by any means I might attain unto the resurrection of the dead.
12 Not as though I had already attained, either were already perfect: but I follow after, if that I may apprehend that for which also I am apprehended of Christ Jesus.

11 if by any means I may attain unto the resur-
12 rection from the dead. Not that I have already
obtained, or am already made perfect; but I press on, if so be that I may [1]lay hold on that for which also I was laid hold on by Christ Jesus.

[1] Or, *lay hold, seeing that also I was laid hold on.*

condition, in which he was learning the fellowship of Christ's sufferings. In this state of constant danger, in which at any moment his fellowship with his Lord in suffering might terminate in his conformity with his very death, it was the apostle's constant prayer that he might endure his trials to the very end in the same spirit as the Master.

11. Here is presented the great final aim of all this experience. The problematical form of expression, **if by any means,** does not imply doubt on the apostle's part, but is simply suggested by his humility. For other examples of this form of expression, see Acts 27 : 12; Rom. 1 : 10; 11 : 14. The resurrection of the dead here referred to is, of course, the first resurrection. (1 Cor. 15 : 23; 1 Thess. 4 : 16.) He says simply the resurrection, not that he did not believe in the resurrection both of the righteous and the wicked, for he expressly taught it (Acts 24 : 15), as did also Christ (John 5 : 28, 29), but because he regarded the resurrection of the good as the only one in which he had any interest. To attain unto this was to reach the fulfillment of all his highest and holiest hopes. What a glorious privilege it will be to rise out of the darkness of the tomb, clothed in a spiritual body which shall be a perfect abode for the immortal spirit, both body and spirit being freed from all sin and delivered forever from the curse under which we now groan! (2 Cor. 5 : 4.)

12. In contrast with his former pride, when as a Pharisee he thought himself blameless, he now humbly disclaims all pretensions to perfection, and simply claims to be striving after it; and he holds up a striking picture of his earnestness in this effort, with a view to encouraging others to like mindedness. **Not as though I had already attained**—better, *not that I have*, etc. (Revised Version). He anticipates the possibility of some one's saying that he is puffed up with self-conceit, and hence adds this disclaimer. After the word 'attained,' Meyer and some others mentally supply the word 'the prize,' and suppose that already the idea of a race had begun to shape the apostle's language; but it is much more natural to suppose that he speaks here without any thought of the race course, and that gradually the figure of the foot race begins to unfold itself. In this case the word to be mentally supplied with attained is "this," or "these things," referring to his previous description of the believer's state. (Ver. 9-11.) "I do not mean," he says, "that I have attained all this." "In his highest fervor the apostle does not lose spiritual sobriety." (Bengel.) The believer's sanctification, even when that believer is such a saint as Paul, is progressive, and is not reached this side the grave. That this idea of perfection is the one in Paul's mind is shown by the words he adds immediately to explain his not having attained. **Either were already perfect.** I have not yet reached such a point that I can say, I am perfect. The twice repeated 'already' emphasizes the idea of the present moment, implying at the same time that what is not yet true will some time be true.[1] **But I follow after**—or, as in Revised Version, *I press on.* The idea of the foot race begins to emerge, though it does not appear distinctly till ver. 14. **If that I may apprehend that for which also[2] I am apprehended of Christ Jesus.** Christ apprehended him on the way to Damascus, and now he follows on to apprehend that for which he had been apprehended, his moral

[1] The first verb 'attained,' refers by its tense to the time of his conversion; the second, 'am made perfect' (Revised Version), brings his condition down to the present moment. I did not attain at the time of my conversion, nor has there been a moment up to the present when I could pronounce myself perfect. The second verb is found nowhere else in Paul's writings, though frequent elsewhere.

[2] The phrase translated 'that for which' in the Common and the Revised Versions is a puzzle to interpreters, and has received various meanings. It may mean as above, or "because," in which case the following clause states the reason. The first gives a more picturesque thought, at least.

13 Brethren, I count not myself to have apprehended: but *this* one thing *I do*, forgetting those things which are behind, and reaching forth unto those things which are before,

14 I press toward the mark for the prize of the high calling of God in Christ Jesus.

15 Let us therefore, as many as be perfect, be thus minded: and if in any thing ye be otherwise minded, God shall reveal even this unto you.

13 Brethren, I count not myself [1]yet to have laid
hold; but one thing *I do*, forgetting the things
which are behind, and stretching forward to the
14 things which are before, I press on toward the goal
unto the prize of the [2]high calling of God in Christ
15 Jesus. Let us therefore, as many as be perfect, be
thus minded: and if in anything ye are otherwise

1 Many ancient authorities omit *yet*......2 Or, *upward*.

and spiritual perfection, which was the purpose Christ had in view when he laid his hand upon him. When he felt the pressure of that divine hand, the apostle turned about and followed eagerly on, to obtain that prize which the Master had in view for him. How well this verb 'apprehend' describes his conversion! It was no quiet invitation that Paul obeyed, like that given to John and Peter, but it was a violent seizure, by which he was arrested in his course.

13. He solemnly and impressively re-affirms his humble opinion of himself, preparatory to a statement of his earnest striving after perfection, and perhaps with the idea of holding up a mirror before the Philippians, some of whom at least seemed inclined to vaingloriousness and pride. See 2 : 3. **Brethren**—when the apostle's feelings are deeply moved, he is apt to use this word—**I count not myself to have apprehended.** "Others might easily think this of Paul." (Bengel.) On a similar emphatic collocation of the words "I," "myself," see John 5 : 30; 7 : 17; 8 : 54; Acts 26 : 9. After repeating in a slightly different form the first words of the previous verse, he proceeds to describe in a highly figurative way his earnest efforts after perfection, which he had described more prosaically in the closing words of ver. 12. The words which he has been using, 'pursue' and 'apprehend,' as yet apparently without any distinct figure in mind, now suggest the beautiful image of the race course, and lead to a striking comparison of himself to a runner in the well-known races. **But this one thing I do.** In the Greek it is very emphatic. 'But one thing'—forgetting, etc. There is no verb corresponding to the words 'I do,' and the mind is led to rest for a moment on the simple words "but one thing" (ἓν δέ), and then passes on to the description that follows, which constitutes the one thing. **Forgetting those things which are behind.** These are not the Jewish distinctions referred to in ver. 5, 6, for these had been already abandoned previous to his entering upon the race; but they are his past experiences, his successes and failures, his good works and his sins alike. All these he leaves behind, yea, even forgets, not of course in such a way as to lose their lessons of encouragement and of warning, but like the runner who thinks not of the ground already trod, but only of that which intervenes between himself and the goal. "The looking back that Paul condemns is that which breaks the pace and lessens the speed." (Calvin.) **And reaching forth**—or, *stretching forward* (Revised Version), a very picturesque word in the Greek, bringing before us the eager, excited runner, with his head and neck extended toward the goal, his ardent spirit outrunning his lagging feet. **Unto those things which are before.** The 'things before' are not the prize, as some suppose, but the attainments in the Christian life which yet lie between his present condition and the final goal of perfection.

14. I press toward the mark—or, *the goal*—**for the prize.** In ancient games this was generally a wreath, hung at the goal. In Paul's case it is that perfection, which he has already disclaimed, but which he will yet attain. This is 'the prize' **of the high calling.** The English word 'calling' suggests vocation, business, but the Greek word has no such double significance. It means simply the call, or act of calling, which is described as high—that is, heavenly (Heb. 3 : 1), because God calls to us from the heavens above. It is 'the prize of the high calling,' because it is that reward "which the heavenly calling holds forth." (Luther.) The figure of the race course is dropped with these words, and the language becomes literal again. **Of God in Christ Jesus**—for God calls us in the person of his Son. (1 Cor. 7 : 22; 1 Peter 5 : 10.)

15. In this and the following verse we have the practical application to the Philippians of this description of his own spirit. **Therefore**—since this spirit is the right spirit to cherish—

16 Nevertheless, whereto we have already attained, let us walk by the same rule, let us mind the same thing.
17 Brethren, be followers together of me, and mark them which walk so as ye have us for an ensample.

16 minded, even this shall God reveal unto you: only, whereunto we have already attained, by that same *rule* let us walk.
17 Brethren, be ye imitators together of me, and mark them who so walk even as ye have us for an

as many as be perfect—not in the sense of attainment, for the apostle's words have already excluded that idea, but of aim and purpose. "Perfect, and not perfect; perfect travelers, not yet perfect possessors." (Augustine.) The perfect on earth are those that seek perfection, and have come in their Christian life to a certain maturity of faith and knowledge, so that they are no longer mere babes in Christ. See Matt. 5 : 48; 1 Cor. 2 : 6; 3 : 1; 14 : 20; Eph. 4 : 13, 14; Col. 4 : 12; Heb. 5 : 14. In this word perfect there may be implied a contrast with those Christians who were still clinging to the things that Paul had discarded, still putting a certain honor on lineage, circumcision, and outward righteousness, and unable wholly to renounce a measure of confidence in such things. In the use of the words 'as many as,' the apostle leaves it to the conscience of each reader or hearer to determine whether he belongs to this class or not. **Be thus minded**—literally, *think this;* that is, which I think. Compare 2 : 5. By these words he means to enjoin upon them that same humble, yet earnest striving after perfection which distinguishes himself. Let this be your thought, as it is mine, not to sit down content with the past, but to press ever onward to the goal. **And if in any thing ye be otherwise[1] minded,** as is probably the case.[2] The difference here spoken of as existing in the case of some is a different frame of mind from that of the apostle and the perfect. Such a divergence is wrong, but with Christian tolerance Paul says, God will also set this right. He does not uncharitably rebuke them for their different spirit, but with a sweet charity looks forward to the time when their eyes will be opened to discover their error. **God shall reveal even this unto you,** as he has revealed other things. God will set you right by his Holy Spirit (Eph. 1 : 17; Col. 1 : 9), and show you the truth concerning that matter in which you now differ from me. In this sweet spirit of tolerance there is a practical lesson for us. We cannot always act or think alike, and in such cases we are not to yield our own opinion or mode of action, if they seem right to us, but to maintain them in charity, waiting for that fuller revelation which shall declare us right and others wrong, or the reverse.

16. The exact shade of thought in this verse it is hard to determine in the original, though the general meaning is plain enough. He will have unity of thought and purpose as far as possible. **Nevertheless**—or, *only* (as in Revised Version); this, and nothing more. **Whereto we have already attained**—whatever Christian progress we have made, both in faith and knowledge. **Let us walk[3] by the same rule, let us mind the same thing.** The last clause is an interpolation, and rightly discarded in the Revised Version. While we wait for fuller revelation, let our present attainments be the rule of our conduct. Walk by the rule of that already received. Do not abandon any present experience, but continue to walk by the light of that until you obtain new light.

17-4 : 1. NECESSITY OF FOLLOWING GOOD EXAMPLES ENFORCED BY A VIVID CONTRAST OF THE CHARACTER AND DESTINY OF FALSE AND TRUE BELIEVERS.—The apostle presses upon their attention his example and that of his imitators (17), and enforces the duty of copying such lives by a vivid picture of the character and fearful destiny of false professors (18, 19), in contrast with the exalted life and glorious destiny of true believers (20, 21), closing with a final exhortation to steadfastness (4 : 1).

17. Brethren, be followers together of me. The word 'brethren' indicates his deep feeling. See ver. 13. The injunction is more clear in the Revised Version. "*Be ye imitators together,*" or *co-imitators*, one and all, "with one consent, with one mind." (Calvin.) Compare 1 Cor. 4 : 16; 11 : 1; 1 Thess. 1 : 6; 2 Thess. 3 : 7, 9. 'Of me.' What a conscious-

[1] The word translated 'otherwise' (ἑτέρως) is found nowhere else in the New Testament.

[2] Εἰ with the indicative assumes the case to be a real one. Winer's "Grammar," §41, b, 2. a; Kühner, §339, 2, 1 (a); Hadley, 745, 1.

[3] The infinitive στοιχεῖν is used as an emphatic imperative, as in Rom. 12 : 15.

18 (For many walk, of whom I have told you often, and now tell you even weeping, *that they are* the enemies of the cross of Christ:
19 Whose end *is* destruction, whose God *is their* belly, and *whose* glory *is* in their shame, who mind earthly things.)

18 ensample. For many walk, of whom I told you often, and now tell you even weeping, *that they are*
19 the enemies of the cross of Christ: whose end is perdition, whose god is the belly, and *whose* glory

ness of duties performed and sins resisted these words imply! He had already disclaimed perfection; in the sight of God he is nothing but a sinner saved by grace. In a still later epistle he even calls himself "chief of sinners" (1 Tim. 1:15), yet, notwithstanding all this, he realizes that in the sight of man he has walked in such obedience that the Philippians can take no better example to copy. Few, indeed, could thus appeal to their own life without thereby bringing to mind some flagrant weakness of character, and so exposing their claims to ridicule. But the Philippians are to copy not only Paul, but those who live as he does. On 'walk,' as denoting a chosen course of life, see ver. 16; Acts 21:24; Rom. 4:12; Gal. 5:25. He does not say those who walk as *they*, but **as ye have us for an ensample,** for he would have the Philippians apply the test, since they knew what his life had been, and whether any others walked in accordance with it or not. "The inferior examples of the friends of Christ's cross should be tried by the standard of the greater and more perfect." (Bengel,) At the same time, by keeping the inferior examples also in view, the Philippians would obtain a more perfect standard than by taking any single life. The example of Timothy, Epaphroditus, and perhaps many others, might add some beautiful traits to their conception of the Christian life, even though that conception had been derived from the contemplation of so glorious a life as that of St. Paul. "There are innumerable models laid before thee in the Scriptures of virtuous lives, so, if you will, go to the disciples after the Master." (Chrysostom.) "We must propound to ourselves the highest pitch and the best patterns of perfection; follow the forwardest Christians with a desire to overtake them; dwell upon their exemplary lives till ye be changed into the same image." (Trapp.) 'Ensample,' in the singular, indicates that the standard is only one, though found in many individuals.

18. The reason why he urges them to keep before their minds the example of the good, is that even many professed Christians live very impure lives. Those here mentioned must have been Christians, not Jews or Gentiles; for otherwise there would be no special appropriateness in the allusion. The Philippians would not have been likely to copy the example of unbelievers; but Paul was very much afraid that they might copy the bad example of these professed disciples. Whether they resided in Philippi or not, we cannot tell, but they were, at least, well known there, for Paul had often spoken to the church about them, and now, in view of their increasing wickedness and pernicious influence, mentions them with tears, and declares them to be **enemies of the cross of Christ.** They are opposed to the doctrine of self-denial, and refuse to accept the cross which every believer must bear. See Matt. 10:38; 16:24; Mark 8:34; Luke 9:23; 14:27. The apostle had just reason to fear their influence, for they perverted that truth which he taught so earnestly, that the Christian is not under the law, but under grace. Such lawless Christians only served to bring that gracious doctrine into discredit. In Romans, ch. 6, he argues at greater length against these perverters of the doctrine of Christian liberty. Compare also Rom. 16:18.

19. The destiny and character of these false professors are painted in lurid colors. For equally severe descriptions of such characters from other apostles, see 2 Peter 2:10-22; Jude 12, 13. **Whose end is destruction.** Bengel well says that this statement of their destiny precedes the description of their character, in order that the latter "may be read with the greater horror." Their end is destruction, separation from the presence of God and confinement in the place of torment. According to the Saviour's words, many who have not only professed faith in him, but also have apparently accomplished great things in his name, will be found among the lost. (Matt. 7:21, seq.) On the word 'end,' compare Rom. 6:21; 2 Cor. 11:15; Heb. 6:8; on "destruction," compare Matt. 7:13; Rom. 9:22. To this description of their destiny Paul now adds a scathing portrayal of their character.

20 For our conversation is in heaven; from whence also we look for the Saviour, the Lord Jesus Christ:
21 Who shall change our vile body, that it may be fashioned like unto his glorious body, according to the working whereby he is able even to subdue all things unto himself.

20 is in their shame, who mind earthly things. For
our [1] citizenship is in heaven; from whence also we
wait for a Saviour, the Lord Jesus Christ: who
21 shall fashion anew the body of our humiliation, *that
it may be* conformed to the body of his glory, according to the working whereby he is able even to subject all things unto himself.

1 Or, *commonwealth.*

Whose God is their belly. They are given up to the worst kind of lusts, and find their chief satisfaction in the gratification of their animal nature. Compare Rom. 16 : 18. Moreover, like the heathen (Rom. 1 : 32), they not only commit abominable sins, but their **glory is in their shame.** They take pride in those very things which in the estimation of the good are really a shame and disgrace; they justify their vices. The last feature of the description—**who mind earthly things**[1]—presents the essentially earthly character of their state of mind and heart; they think of nothing but earthly matters, have no high and heavenly thoughts and aspirations, but concentrate their whole soul upon the things of time and sense. Paul in Romans, ch. 8, describes most beautifully the opposite frame of mind, which is characteristic of the true Christian.

20. The opposite character and destiny of true believers, "in outlines few, but how clear." **Our** is placed first in the Greek with emphasis—'ours' in contrast with theirs. **Conversation** (or, as in Revised Version, *citizenship*). The former translation is taken from the Vulgate (*conversatio*), and signifies, according to ancient English usage, manner of life, behavior,—not discourse. This last conception, which is probably that of the ordinary reader, suggests the beautiful idea that the Christian thinks and talks chiefly of heavenly things—an idea undoubtedly implied in the correct rendering, for it is the natural contrast to "minding earthly things," but still it is not an accurate interpretation either of the English word 'conversation' in the Common Version, or of the original Greek word. That Greek term has various significations, which are very closely related, commonwealth, country, citizenship, but not conversation, in the modern sense of that word. Paul reminds his readers that their true commonwealth, or citizenship, is above, not on earth. The true Christian, like Abraham, seeks no continuing city here, for he is a stranger and pilgrim on earth, and his real country is the heavenly. In Heb. 11 : 13-16 we have a most beautiful unfolding of this idea of our heavenly citizenship. Compare also Eph. 2 : 19. "We live by the same laws as saints and angels do. . . . While we live by heaven's laws, and go about our earthly business with heavenly minds; this a carnal mind cannot skill of." (Trapp.) "With the body we walk about on earth, with the heart we dwell in heaven." (Augustine.) From this heaven, where our true home is, **we look for the Saviour.** In the Greek, 'Saviour' is placed first, and separated from its related words, its isolated position giving it great emphasis. The verb translated 'look for' is a picturesque word, suggesting the idea of waiting with expectation and eagerness until the wished-for object comes. Compare Rom. 8 : 23, 25; 1 Cor. 1 : 7; Gal. 5 : 5.

21. In describing the fearful destiny of false believers, Paul used only one trenchant word 'destruction,' but he dwells longer upon the glorious destiny of believers, which he pictures from the standpoint of the resurrection, because in his mind that involves all the rest. The Common Version has gone astray in its translation **our vile body,** there being nothing in the original corresponding to the adjective 'vile.' It was not a principle of Paul's philosophy to despise the body, nor does Christianity give any countenance to the ancient Greek notion of the essential vileness and worthlessness of the flesh, but rather teaches us to look for the redemption of the body, as well as of the soul, from the taint of sin and the bondage of corruption. The proper translation of these words is that of the Revised Version, "the body of our humiliation," which Paul so describes, because in it

[1] On the change in the construction of the last clause, for the sake of emphasis, see Winer, §59, 8, b; §62, 3; Buttmann, §123, 5.

CHAPTER IV.

THEREFORE, my brethren dearly beloved and longed for, my joy and crown, so stand fast in the Lord, *my* dearly beloved.
2 I beseech Euodias, and beseech Syntyche, that they be of the same mind in the Lord.

1 Wherefore, my brethren beloved and longed for, my joy and crown, so stand fast in the Lord, my beloved.
2 I exhort Euodia, and I exhort Syntyche, to be of

we experience those painful and humiliating experiences, privations, afflictions, persecutions, which belong to the Christian life on earth. This body, in which now we are so often humiliated, is to be changed at Christ's coming, and fashioned **like unto his glorious body** (or, *the body of his glory*), that body which he possesses in his glorified state, for, as John says (1 Epistle 3:2), "we shall be like him." Compare Rom. 8: 29; 1 Cor. 15: 49. It is the fashion of the body only that will be changed, as suggested by the word here used (μετασχηματίσει), and its identity will be preserved, as Paul plainly teaches in 1 Cor. 15: 37, by the analogy of the seed; though of course we cannot understand either the nature of the change or the relation of the present body to that future one. All this great change is to be effected **according to the working** (or, *energy*) of that almighty ability, **whereby he is able even to subdue all things unto himself.** "It is the work of the Lord's omnipotence." (Bengel.) This supreme ability of the Saviour is dwelt upon more fully in Col. 1: 16, seq., and is referred to in Heb. 1: 3. That power by which Christ can subject all things unto himself is an unassailable evidence of his ability to change our bodies from humiliation to glory.

Ch. 4. CONCLUSION OF THE PRECEDING EXHORTATION WHICH SHOULD PROPERLY FORM A PART OF THE PREVIOUS CHAPTER.

1. In conclusion, the apostle tenderly and fervently exhorts them to maintain a spirit of unity. The vision of future glory suggested at the close of the previous chapter should be a present inspiration. So at the close of the great chapter on the resurrection Paul transmutes that sublime vision of future glory into an inspiring force in the present. (1 Cor. 15: 58.) **My brethren,** etc. This accumulation of affectionate epithets springs from his loving heart, which is especially moved by the remembrance of this well ordered church. "They are not terms of flattery, but of sincere love." (Calvin.) In no other Epistle do we find such numerous expressions of affectionate praise. **Dearly beloved and longed for.**[1] He not only loves them, but earnestly desires to see them again. "What heart-melting language is here! Ministers must woo hard for Christ, and speak fair, if they will speak to purpose." (Trapp.) **Joy and crown.** Such disciples not only give him the greatest joy, but crown his ministry with an imperishable wreath of glory. Compare the similar words in 1 Thess. 2: 19. **So stand fast**—that is, as those who possess a commonwealth in heaven and are expecting thence the Saviour's coming. **In the Lord.** Nothing can be rightly done except in the Lord, in his strength and grace. **Dearly beloved.** He lingers on these loving words, as if they had a peculiar sweetness. "This is twice used very sweetly: first, at the beginning of the period, and then for strengthening the exhortation." (Bengel.) The rest of this chapter contains certain general exhortations and final messages which have been well described as "the ethical miscellany with which the apostle often concludes an Epistle."

2, 3. ADMONITIONS TO AND COMMENDATIONS OF CERTAIN INDIVIDUALS.—He urges two women who had become alienated to be at peace (2), and beseeches some well-known associate in the church to assist them in their efforts after harmony (3).

2. I beseech Euodias, and beseech Syntyche. Both of the persons here addressed were evidently women, as appears by the feminine pronoun in ver. 3, which can properly refer only to them. The Common Version translates the first name **Euodias,** as if it were the name of a man; it should be *Euodia*, as in Revised Version. Both names occur in ancient inscriptions, but are found nowhere else in the New Testament. These women were probably ladies of high character and

[1] The word translated 'longed for," ἐπιπόθητοι, is not found elsewhere in the New Testament.

3 And I entreat thee also, true yokefellow, help those women which laboured with me in the gospel, with Clement also, and *with* other my fellow labourers, whose names *are* in the book of life.

3 the same mind in the Lord. Yea, I beseech thee also, true yokefellow, help these women, for they laboured with me in the gospel, with Clement also, and the rest of my fellow-workers, whose names are in the book of life.

position in the church, who had for some reason, to us unknown, become estranged. We learn from Paul's words, that they had been specially helpful to him in times past, but nothing further is known concerning them. Their previous helpfulness increased the apostle's anxiety to see them at peace again. In this difficulty between these two women we may, perhaps, discover the clue to those frequent and earnest exhortations to unity. See 1 : 27; 2 : 2-4, 14; 3 : 15; 4 : 1. The repetition of the verb 'I beseech . . . and beseech,' suggests that Paul would address the same appeal to each one separately, not necessarily that he divides the blame equally between them. He does not exhort one to be reconciled to the other, but each to enter upon the work of reconciliation. "He uses this word [beseech] as if exhorting them singly, face to face, and that most impartially." (Bengel.) **That they be of the same mind in the Lord.** Observe the words again, 'in the Lord,' for Paul can conceive of no goodness apart from Christ; these parties are not only to be reconciled, but in a Christian spirit.

3. And I entreat thee also, true yokefellow. He appeals to a third party to help on this reconciliation; and this appeal shows how strongly the apostle desires it. The verb translated 'entreat' (ἐρωτῶ) shows that he asks as an equal from an equal, while 'ask' (αἰτέω) would suggest the request of an inferior to a superior. (Matt. 7 : 9; Acts 12 : 20.) 'True yokefellow.' These words have been a perpetual stumbling block to commentators, and very varied explanations have been offered of their meaning. Some have supposed that he refers to one of his fellow workers, Luke, Timothy, Silas, Epaphroditus, etc., while some have even supposed the apostle's wife to be referred to. The last suggestion is opposed by grammar for the word is masculine, and by the apostle's clear statement in 1 Cor. 7 : 8, while the first suggestion is not in accordance with Paul's usual method of addressing his fellow laborers; and there would also seem to be an invidious distinction in singling out any individual as a true or genuine 'yokefellow.' Meyer has revived the explanation suggested by Chrysostom as the opinion of some in his day, that the word is a proper name, Syzygus. With this explanation, which seems probable in view of the fact that all the rest here referred to are mentioned by name, all the difficulties easily vanish. We should simply have the name revealed of another, and otherwise unknown laborer in Philippi, who was evidently greatly trusted by the apostle; in which case the use of the adjective would become eminently proper, "true, genuine, Syzygus," that is, rightly so named, there being a graceful play upon his name, as in the case of Onesimus. See Philem. 11. The only objection to this view, and it does not seem very decisive, is the fact that such a name has never been discovered anywhere else. **Those women,** rather '*them.*' The Common Version overlooks, or at least obscures, the reference of the pronoun to Euodia and Syntyche, but it is no new case the apostle is here considering. He is simply adding to his personal appeal to the women themselves, a request that Syzygus would aid them in their efforts at reconciliation, and to emphasize his request, he characterizes these women as persons who had been of great service to himself personally.[1] They had labored with him most likely, when he founded the church in Philippi, where, it may be remembered, the gospel was first preached to a company of women, and Lydia, the first convert, had opened her house to the apostles, and gathered the church for worship under her roof. (Acts 16 : 13, 15, 40.) "It is proper to help a person who once stood well, even when he is wavering." (Bengel.) "All men should contribute their help to the composing of differences, and bring their buckets, as it were, to quench this unnatural fire, when once kindled." (Trapp.) The verb suggests that the labors which these women had shared with the apostle, had involved some severe toil and suffering. He uses the same verb in 1 : 27. **With**

[1] The pronoun suggests that what follows is in the nature of a reason, "as being persons who." See Liddell and Scott's "Greek Lexicon"; Hadley's "Greek Grammar," section 681, b.

4 Rejoice in the Lord always: *and* again I say, Rejoice.
5 Let your moderation be known unto all men. The Lord *is* at hand.

4 Rejoice in the Lord alway; again I will say, Re-
5 joice. Let your [1] forbearance be known unto all

[1] Or, *gentleness*.

Clement also. Clement was for a long time supposed to be the famous Clement of Rome, author of an "Epistle to the Corinthians," and Roman Catholic expositors still maintain that view, but most others have either abandoned it, or entertain it as a mere possibility. The probabilities are altogether against any such identification of persons. Whoever he was, he had made himself conspicuously useful to Paul, so that he was constrained to honor him by name. **With other my fellow-labourers.** Of this unnamed remainder of his helpers he beautifully says, **whose names are in the book of life.** Unnamed by him, they are all named there. Paul inferred this fact from what he had seen of their Christian life and character, "the seals of that undisclosed election." (Calvin.) For the origin of that phrase 'book of life;' compare Exodus 32:32; Psalm 69:28; Isaiah 4:3; Ezek. 13:9; Dan. 12:1; Luke 10:20.

4-9. FINAL AND GENERAL EXHORTATION. He exhorts them to joyfulness (4), gentleness (5), contentment (6), with the promise of the peace of God as the result (7), and finally enjoins spiritual mindedness (8), and obedience to all his instructions (9).

4. Rejoice. This injunction, which he has once before used at 3:1, again takes up the thread which was broken off by the long digression, 3:2-4:3, ringing out once more the keynote of the Epistle. See on 1:4. **In the Lord.** Again appears this characteristic phrase, so peculiar to Paul. He adds also the word **always,** because Christians should not only rejoice, but rejoice under all circumstances, no matter what sacrifices they have to make, what trials to bear, what losses to sustain, for all these are part of the divine plan in accordance with which all things work together for good to God's people. (Rom. 8:28.) See 1 Cor. 3:21, seq.; 2 Cor. 6:10; 1 Thess. 5:16. In Rom. 5:1-5, Paul states most beautifully the reasons for such joy, even in the most unfavorable circumstances—in prison, in this very city of Philippi, he had himself most signally illustrated his injunction to rejoice always. See Acts 16:25. **Again I say**—rather, *will say* (ἐρῶ, future). So earnest is Paul in enforcing this duty, that he repeats the very same word 'rejoice.' "Well has he repeated the word, for since the nature of things produces grief, he shows by repeating that they should by all means rejoice." (Chrysostom.)

5. Moderation—rather, "forbearance" (Revised Version), or "gentleness" (margin of Revised Version). It is that quality which leads one to yield rather than to insist on the full measure of his rights, to suffer wrong rather than to do wrong, "as holding utmost right to be utmost wrong." It was characteristic of Christ beyond all others (2 Cor. 10:1), and of Paul especially among the apostles. This mildness of temper they should make so conspicuous a feature of their character that it should come to **be known unto all men,** with whom they might come into contact. The injunction was specially appropriate in the days of persecution, when they might have been tempted to exhibit harshness of temper. To enforce this injunction he adds the words, **the Lord is at hand,** who will right all wrongs, and reward all fidelity. Many have inferred from such expressions as this that Paul expected Christ's Second Coming in his own lifetime, or at least in the lifetime of the existing generation; but in 2 Thess. 2:2 he expressly disclaims any such interpretation of his words. From that passage we learn that Paul did not *teach* any such doctrine, while in Acts 1:7 we are taught by the Lord himself that the time of his Second Coming was not to be revealed even to inspired apostles. If, however, it be said that Paul evidently believed the Lord's coming to be near, even if he did not expressly teach it, and that such expectation colored his language, we reply that Paul could just as consistently employ the language he uses, even if he thought the day to be very distant; for practically the Lord is at hand for every one of us—the day of one's death is actually for him the coming of Christ to judgment. "It is appointed unto men once to die, but after this the judgment" (Heb. 9:27); after death the next great

6 Be careful for nothing; but in everything by prayer and supplication with thanksgiving let your requests be made known unto God.
7 And the peace of God, which passeth all understanding, shall keep your hearts and minds through Christ Jesus.

6 men. The Lord is at hand. In nothing be anxious; but in everything by prayer and supplication with thanksgiving let your requests be made known unto
7 God. And the peace of God, which passeth all understanding, shall guard your hearts and your thoughts in Christ Jesus.

event in the drama of life is the judgment. However long an interval may separate the two, they are practically close together. If one, therefore, lived in the constant presence of this thought, as Paul lived, he might be stirred by the expectation of Christ's coming to judgment, even though it seemed to him an event of the far distant future. See 1 : 6.

6. **Be careful for nothing**—with an anxious carefulness. The Greek word implies a care that divides and distracts the mind, as in Christ's well-known injunction in Matt. 6 : 34. It is an outgrowth of that spirit which ever looks solicitously forward, and forgets to-day's blessings and duties in anxieties about to-morrow's claims. "It is possible to sink below this anxiety in mere levity and thoughtlessness; it is possible to rise above it by casting our care on him who careth for us." 'Nothing' is placed first in the Greek with emphasis, excluding absolutely every subject of anxiety. In opposition to this anxious carefulness, he prescribes the remedy, which is entire confidence in God. Compare 1 Peter 5 : 7. "This is the best cure of care." (Trapp.) **In every thing,** that may happen, in emphatic contrast by its position in the sentence with the 'nothing' of the previous clause. **By prayer and supplication.** These words are joined together also in Eph. 6 : 18; 1 Tim. 2 : 1; 5 : 5. The first is the more general term, including adoration, thanksgiving, etc.; the second is the more specific, designating a single feature of prayer, petition for necessities. "Prayer and care are more opposite than water and fire." (Bengel.) **With thanksgiving.** Supplication for mercies should ever go hand in hand with thanksgiving for past favors. See 1 Thess. 5 : 18; 1 Tim. 2 : 1. "We should come to pray with our thanks in our hands, standing ready with it, as Joseph's brethren stood with their present. Prayer goes up without incense when without thankfulness." (Trapp.) **Requests** — literally, *things asked for* (αἰτήματα). **Be made known** —though they are already known (Matt. 6 : 8), for it is the will of God that we should ask for what we need. **Unto God**—literally, *before God* (πρὸς τὸν θεόν); before whose throne your petitions are laid. Some one has aptly turned Paul's injunction into an epigram: "Be careful for nothing, be prayerful for everything, be thankful for anything."

7. The result of such a spirit of prayer will be the possession of a wonderful peace, the peace of God, "the image of God's own tranquillity." Prayer may not always be answered in the way we expect, but always as the result of true prayer there will come this immeasurable blessing. This is not the peace of reconciliation, the "peace with God" of Rom. 5 : 1; but the peace of trust, the repose of a believing heart, which Christ so beautifully describes in John 14 : 27, and which presupposes the peace of reconciliation as its foundation. This repose of spirit Paul describes most eloquently as **the peace of God which passeth all**— or, rather, *every*—**understanding;** that is, the power of every mind to comprehend it. No human mind is adequate to understand or estimate this peace. Compare Eph. 3 : 19. "He who possesses it has more than he himself knows; more than he can express in word or thought." **Shall keep**—or, rather, as in Revised Version, "shall guard" (φρουρήσει). Compare 2 Cor. 11 : 32. By a military metaphor Paul represents this peace as keeping guard over and protecting their hearts, as a garrison holds a fortress. At every inlet into their souls this peace stands like an armed sentinel, keeping out all disturbing influences. "Solomon's bed was not so well guarded with his threescore valiant men, all holding swords (Canticles 3 : 7, 8), as each good Christian is by the power of God without him, and the peace of God within him." (Trapp.) **Your hearts and minds**—or, better, *thoughts*, as in Revised Version. 'Hearts' and thoughts are here connected together, because, according to the Biblical conception, "the heart is the seat of the thoughts." (Bengel.) See Matt. 12 : 34; 15 : 19, etc. The peace of God keeps the heart and the thoughts issuing from it serene and calm. How different this condition from the ceaseless anxieties of the world (Matt. 6 : 31, 32), or its false security (1 Thess. 5 : 3)! **Through**—

8 Finally, brethren, whatsoever things are true, whatsoever things *are* honest, whatsoever things *are* just, whatsoever things *are* pure, whatsoever things *are* lovely, whatsoever things *are* of good report; if *there be* any virtue, and if *there be* any praise, think on these things.

9 Those things, which ye have both learned, and received, and heard, and seen in me, do: and the God of peace shall be with you.

8 Finally, brethren, whatsoever things are true,
whatsoever things are [1] honourable, whatsoever things
are just, whatsoever things are pure, whatsoever things
are lovely, whatsoever things are of [2] good report; if
there be any virtue, and if there be any praise,
9 [3] think on these things. The things which ye both
learned and received and heard and saw in me, these
things do: and the God of peace shall be with you.

1 Gr. *reverend*......2 Or, *gracious* ......3 Gr. *take account of*.

rather, *in*—**Christ Jesus,** in union with whom this divine guardianship is alone experienced.

8. Finally. Here we have 'finally' again (see 3 : 1), actually bringing in this time the concluding portion of the Epistle. In the following sentence, beautiful in its rhythm and impressive in its sententious brevity, we have a noble demand for Christian thinking and Christian living. The sixfold repetition of **whatsoever** (ὅσα) adds much to the impressiveness of the sentence. See Buttmann's "New Testament Grammar," p. 398. **True** are here things not speculative, but practical; for the practical character of the whole admonition shows that truth in conduct is meant. "Virtue is true, vice is falsehood." (Chrysostom.) Compare John 3 : 21; 1 Cor. 5 : 8; Eph. 5 : 9; 1 John 1 : 6. Truth in speech and conduct Paul places, first of all, in the list of moral excellencies. **Honest** is here used in the old English sense of the word, 'honorable,' which is very nearly the meaning of the Greek word (σεμνά). It is whatever is venerable and sacred in character, worthy of honor in the sight of God and men. Compare 1 Tim. 2 : 2; Titus 2 : 2. **Just**—in accordance with eternal and unchangeable righteousness (δικαιοσύνη). **Pure**—not simply chaste, but, as Calvin well says, it "denotes purity in all the relations of life." Compare 1 Tim. 5 : 22; James 3 : 17; 1 John 3 : 3. **Lovely**—calculated to produce love in a well-ordered heart. "There is nothing more lovable than virtue." (Cicero.) From the true standpoint, immorality is hateful. **Of good report**—not, "well spoken of," but as Luther correctly translates it, "that which sounds well"; and hence, winning, attractive.[1] The apostle now sums up all these various features of moral conduct, and any others that might be thought of, in a phrase that covers the whole range of moral excellencies. **If there be any virtue, and if there be any praise.** 'Virtue' is used nowhere else by Paul, and is found only in 1 Peter 2 : 9; 2 Peter 1 : 3, 5, in the New Testament. Paul probably does not shrink from this term, as some suppose, because it is essentially a heathenish word, unworthy of Christianity, but because he preferred to dwell upon the more specific designations of moral excellence, just as he also preferred to describe wickedness under its specific forms, rather than by some general term. Compare Col. 3 : 8, 12. By 'virtue' here he means moral goodness in itself; by 'praise,' such goodness reflected in the speech and writings of men. Thus Christ's commendation of humility; Paul's of charity, would answer to the meaning of 'praise.' **Think on these things**—take to heart, so as to govern your lives accordingly. We grow like our thoughts; we cannot entertain impure thoughts without becoming corrupt, and we cannot think good thoughts without becoming pure. "Meditation precedes, and work follows." (Calvin.) "To restore a commonplace truth to its first uncommon lustre, we need only translate it into action. But to do this you must have reflected on its truth." (Coleridge.)

9. To this injunction to cherish pure and right thoughts, he adds an incentive to right action from his own speech and example. **Those things which ye have both learned, and received**—that is, from him as a teacher. The word 'received' differs from 'learned' by suggesting assent to the teaching. Compare 1 Cor. 15 : 1. **And heard, and seen in me**—as an example. The first verb does not refer to reports of his conduct that had come to their ears, but to his conduct as evinced in words, so that the two verbs describe his conduct in words and deeds; the first they had 'heard,' the second they had 'seen.' **Do**—not simply ponder, but practice. That must be a noble and blameless life which could justify

[1] The Greek words προσφιλῆ, 'lovely,' and εὔφημα, 'of good report,' occur nowhere else in the New Testament.

10 But I rejoiced in the Lord greatly, that now at the last your care of me hath flourished again; wherein ye were also careful, but ye lacked opportunity.
11 Not that I speak in respect of want: for I have learned, in whatsoever state I am, *therewith* to be content.

10 But I [1] rejoice in the Lord greatly that now at
length ye have revived your thought for me;
[2] wherein ye did indeed take thought, but ye lacked
11 opportunity. Not that I speak in respect of want:
for I have learned, in whatsoever state I am, therein

1 Gr. *rejoiced*.......2 Or, *seeing that*.

one in pointing to it as a standard for others. Deficiencies and inconsistencies, which might remain half forgotten, are brought vividly to remembrance by anything like boasting. But the great apostle evidently had no cause to fear any such result, but dared, on all occasions, appeal to the unswerving fidelity of his life and teachings to the precepts of Christ. Compare Acts 20 : 31-35. **And the God of peace shall be with you**—as the result of such a life of pure thoughts and right actions.

10-20. ACKNOWLEDGMENT OF THE GIFTS RECEIVED FROM THE CHURCH.—He compliments them most gracefully and delicately on their thoughtful care for his wants (10), although asserting at the same time his independence (11) and contentment, under all circumstances, through the Lord's gracious aid (13). Nevertheless, they have exhibited the right spirit (14), in striking contrast with other churches (15), more than once (16). Again, declaring that the spirit of the giver is more than the gift itself (17), he expresses his entire satisfaction (18), promises God's blessing upon them in turn (19), and closes with a doxology (20).

10. The apostle now passes to a new topic, as is indicated by the word translated **but** (δέ). This new topic is his grateful acknowledgment of the aid received from the Philippians, which he expresses in most tender and graceful language. **I rejoiced in the Lord**—"not with a worldly joy." (Chrysostom.) Paul rejoices 'in the Lord' over every blessing, whether spiritual or temporal. In everything he beholds the ruling hand of Divine Providence. Compare Acts 28 : 15. **Greatly**—not on account of the gift, but of the Spirit it revealed. **That now at the last**—or, better, as in Revised Version, *now at length*. The words indicate a long interval since their last contribution to his support. **Your care of me hath flourished again.** The Revised Version translates: "Ye have revived your thought for me." The Greek verb is best taken transitively, which is the current usage of the Septuagint. Compare Buttmann, p. 263. In the depth of his feeling the apostle breaks out into poetry. The image before his mind is a tree or plant which has been barren, as in winter time, and then puts forth fresh leaves or flowers. The Philippians had been barren of all care of him for a long time, but now they were blossoming again with thoughts for his comfort. In all this there is no rebuke or reproach, as Chrysostom and others have supposed, every suggestion of which is removed by the very next words. Had not these words been added, there would undoubtedly have been a tone of reproach in the statement, but the whole sentence must be kept in mind. The apostle hastens so quickly to remove every semblance of rebuke from his words, that we are not authorized to find anything of the kind by leaving out the modifying words. His words are very expressive. **Wherein ye were also careful, but ye lacked opportunity.**[1] He declares that this barrenness was due to no lack of love, but of opportunities. Thus the first statement, which seemed, when standing alone, slightly reproachful, is turned into a delicate compliment, which possesses all the more force by the way in which it has been introduced. The visit of Epaphroditus to Rome furnished the Philippians with their long wished for opportunity.

11. Not that I speak in respect of want, etc. The apostle's natural independence asserts itself characteristically in the denial that any personal satisfaction with the material gift prompts this display of gratitude. Not for a moment would he be thought to be so demonstrative over his own renewed comforts. He was no stranger to want, and had learned long ago to think but little about his bodily state. Proudly he says of himself, **for I have learned to be content.** The personal pronoun is used with special emphasis: 'I,' however it may be with others. Have learned "in Christ's school, for nature teacheth

[1] The verb ἠκαιρεῖσθε, 'ye lacked opportunity,' is a late and rare word, found only here in the New Testament.

12 I know both how to be abased, and I know how to abound: every where and in all things I am instructed both to be full and to be hungry, both to abound and to suffer need.

13 I can do all things through Christ which strengtheneth me.

14 Notwithstanding, ye have well done, that ye did communicate with my affliction.

12 to be content. I know how to be abased, and I know
also how to abound: in every thing and in all
things have I learned the secret both to be filled and
13 to be hungry, both to abound and to be in want. I
can do all things in him that strengtheneth me.
14 Howbeit ye did well, that ye had fellowship with

---

no such lesson." (Trapp.) **In whatsoever state**—not only now, but always; a bold statement, yet justified by all we know of the apostle's life. The Greek word (αὐτάρκης) is not exactly translated by 'content,' and in fact there is no exact English word for it. It expresses the idea of self-sufficiency, independence of all external resources. Socrates declared that this was nature's wealth. Many have been as independent as Paul, but few have combined with it such delicate appreciation of the kindness of others. This ability to be independent, and, at the same time, to accept proffered kindness with overflowing gratitude, is one of many proofs that Paul was a most rarely endowed man.

12. He now amplifies the thought just expressed. **I know how to be abased**—that is, to submit to straitened circumstances. He speaks of this first, as the more frequent experience in his own life. The repetition of 'I know' reveals his deep feeling. **How to abound**—that is, how to conduct myself in the midst of plenty, a higher virtue than the other, and harder to acquire. Very few have exhibited both virtues, a becoming spirit of resignation in narrow circumstances, and a noble and generous temper in abundance. Paul's abundance was probably meagre enough, but the same spirit which taught him to make a right use of his slender means would have kept him true amid the glories of Solomon's palace. **Everywhere and in all things.** He desires to emphasize this declaration of complete contentment and therefore adds several amplifying clauses. The Revised Version translates this, "In every thing and in all things"; that is, in every case individually, and in all cases collectively. **I am instructed,** better *have learned the secret.* (Revised Version.) The verb (μεμύημαι) means literally "to be initiated," and contains an allusion to the ancient mysteries, to which only the initiated were admitted. By the use of this word Paul would intimate, as Bengel says, that he was instructed "by a secret discipline unknown to the world." The secret of contentment has become his, not by nature, but by grace.

13. I can do all things through Christ which strengtheneth me. He thus traces back this ability to be independent of circumstances to its true source, the indwelling Christ. It is the grace of Christ that strengthens him, and enables him, not only to exhibit this spirit of contentment, but to 'do all things' that may be necessary in the line of duty. How brief, how noble this utterance! There was nothing, no possible experience, for which Paul did not feel himself adequate, in the strength which Christ imparts. Compare 2 Cor. 12:9; Eph. 6:10; 1 Tim. 1:12; 2 Tim. 2:1; 4:17.

14. As his natural independence has compelled him to defend himself from the suspicion of caring too much for the material gift, so his inbred courtesy leads him to obviate any imputation of slighting their offering. "We may remark how prudently and cautiously he conducts himself on both sides, lest he should incline too much to either. He had descanted magnificently upon his constancy, for he wished the Philippians to beware of thinking that he had given way under the pressure of want. He now takes care, lest from his undaunted manner of speaking, he should appear to have despised their kindness, which would have been a proof not simply of ill breeding and haughtiness, but even of pride." (Calvin.)

Notwithstanding—that is, in spite of my perfect contentment and ability to do without such aid—**ye have well done** in bestowing your gifts, because in so doing, **ye did communicate,** better, *had fellowship,* **with my affliction**—that is, helped him bear his affliction by this practical manifestation of sympathy. It is a characteristically delicate way of describing their act of kindness. He would have them understand that by taking his needs upon their hearts they have practically fellowshiped, or shared, his affliction, and so

15 Now ye Philippians know also, that in the beginning of the gospel, when I departed from Macedonia, no church communicated with me as concerning giving and receiving, but ye only.
16 For even in Thessalonica ye sent once and again unto my necessity.
17 Not because I desire a gift: but I desire fruit that may abound to your account.
18 But I have all, and abound: I am full, having

15 my affliction. And ye yourselves also know, ye
Philippians, that in the beginning of the gospel,
when I departed from Macedonia, no church had
fellowship with me in the matter of giving and re-
16 ceiving, but ye only; for even in Thessalonica ye
17 sent once and again unto my need. Not that I seek
for the gift; but I seek for the fruit that increaseth
18 to your account. But I have all things, and abound:

have lessened the burden of it for the apostle himself.

15. The Philippians have not only mintered to him on this occasion, but also on previous occasions. The direct address, **ye Philippians,** is introduced with affectionate interest. **In the beginning of the gospel**—that is, at the time of their first acquaintance with it, they showed this same spirit of benevolence, in remarkable and beautiful contrast with the rest of the churches he had founded. "They might have said, We will do it, if others have done it: now their praise is the greater; that of the others, the less." (Bengel.) **Communicated with me**—better, "*had fellowship with me.*" (Revised Version.) They had entered into a kind of spiritual partnership with him. **As concerning**—or, *in the matter of*—**giving and receiving.** The words translated 'giving and receiving' are technical terms derived from the language of bookkeeping, but we are not for a moment to suppose that any actual account was kept by Paul or by the Philippians. It is simply the apostle's imaginative way of expressing his sense of obligation. Even as an infant church they had begun to contribute to his wants in such a way as to suggest to his vivid imagination a sort of ledger account between them and himself, in which was contained on the one side the spiritual blessings they had received, and on the other the material gifts he had received. No other church had ever suggested any such necessity for keeping an account of debit and credit, for with them it had been all receipts and no gifts. This was the only church in which mutual services had been rendered. It was doubtless the willing spirit of the Philippians which led Paul to make an exception in their case to the rule he seems to have adopted to accept no support from the churches among which he labored. See 1 Cor. 9:18; 1 Thess. 2:9; 2 Thess. 3:8. He did not forget under other circumstances to refer to this liberality of the Philippian Church. See 2 Cor. 8:2; 9:9. Paley in his "Horae Paulinæ," chapter vii, No. iii, well brings out the undesigned coincidences' between the history and Paul's epistles in this matter of the contribution.

16. For even in Thessalonica, etc. He now emphasizes the statement that the Philippians had shown this spirit from the beginning, by recalling an earlier instance of their generosity. Not only had they contributed to his aid when he departed from Macedonia, but even before that, while he was still in the province, at the neighboring city of Thessalonica, on two different occasions. Well might Paul boast of this church to the Corinthians (see preceding verse), since they formed such a striking contrast with all others. And yet how sad a picture of selfishness and ingratitude we have here painted by the apostle in the praise he bestows upon this one church. Their example appears so bright only by its contrast with the prevailing selfishness. The hardest and most penurious of modern churches, doling out mere pittances to their pastors, shine luminously by the side of the very best churches of apostolic days.

17. Not because I desire a gift. Again, as in ver. 11, the apostle's sensitive heart seeks to clear itself of all suspicion of anything like mercenary motives in this overflowing praise. It is not the 'gift' he cares for, but something higher, even the spiritual blessings which such giving brings to the givers. These blessings are conceived of as **fruit,** which they will gather in the great harvest day. Compare Matt. 25:34, seq., where the Saviour represents himself as specially commending and rewarding such acts at that last day. The repetition of the words **I desire** is emphatic. I do not desire the 'gift,' but I *do* desire the 'fruit.' **That may abound to your account.** "God keeps an exact account of every penny laid out upon him and his, that he may requite it, and his retributions are more than bountiful." (Trapp.)

18. But I have all, and abound. So generously have the Philippians contributed that

received of Epaphroditus the things *which were sent* from you, an odour of a sweet smell, a sacrifice acceptable, well pleasing to God.

19 But my God shall supply all your need according to his riches in glory by Christ Jesus.

20 Now unto God and our Father *be* glory for ever and ever. Amen.

21 Salute every saint in Christ Jesus. The brethren which are with me greet you.

22 All the saints salute you, chiefly they that are of Cæsar's household.

I am filled, having received from Epaphroditus the
things *that came* from you, an odour of a sweet
smell, a sacrifice acceptable, well-pleasing to God.
19 And my God shall supply every need of yours ac-
20 cording to his riches in glory in Christ Jesus. Now
unto [1] our God and Father *be* the glory [2] for ever
and ever. Amen.
21 Salute every saint in Christ Jesus. The brethren
22 who are with me salute you. All the saints salute,
you, especially they that are of Cæsar's household.

1 Or, *God and our Father*......2 Gr. *unto the ages of the ages.*

he has 'all' that he needs, and even more, for he 'abounds.' "The sum they had sent him was undoubtedly not large; yet, moderate as it was, it abounded, he says, to the full satisfying of his wants and of his wishes." (Calvin.) "Behold the contented and grateful mind!" (Bengel.) **I am full** repeats the previous statement in another form. Alluding again to the gift received through Epaphroditus, the apostle describes it as a sweet and acceptable offering to God himself, so putting the final touch to the picture of their kindness. Thus the Philippians have the satisfaction of knowing that their ministration to the apostle's necessities has proved a most perfect and acceptable sacrifice to God on high. See Heb. 13 : 16.

19. And this God, whose servant they have ministered to, will supply all their needs, spiritual and temporal. They have supplied the apostle's bodily necessities, and he can only thank them, but God will requite them in a very different way. **He shall supply all your needs**—not as they have supplied the apostle's,—out of their poverty,—but **according to his riches in glory**—that is, his glorious inexhaustible resources. "It is easy to him." (Chrysostom.) Meyer takes the words 'in glory' as belonging to the verb, "He will supply in glory"; that is, in heaven. But the combination of the words 'riches in glory' is grammatical, and yields the better sense; namely, that God will reward the Philippians for their generosity, both in this world and the world to come, out of his infinitely glorious riches. **By** (Revised Version, *in*) **Christ Jesus**—in union with whom alone is any one an object of the divine favor and blessing.

20. The thought of God leads the apostle to break forth into a doxology, with which this section fittingly concludes. **Now unto God and our Father** (literally, as in Revised Version, "our God and Father," for the Greek word 'our' belongs to both nouns.) 'God' expresses the natural relation of the Deity to us, 'Father' his relation to us in Christ. (Rom. 8 : 15; Gal. 4 : 5.) **Be glory for ever and ever** (literally, *to ages of ages*)—an imitation of the Hebrew.

21-23. SALUTATIONS AND BENEDICTIONS.—He sends a salutation to every saint, together with the greeting of the brethren at Rome (21), especially of the household of Caesar (22), and closes with a benediction. (23.)

21. Salute. This is probably addressed to the immediate recipients of the letter, the bishops and deacons, who are to 'salute' the brethren at Philippi in the apostle's name. **Every saint.** "The singular individualizes—every saint individually." (Bengel.) 'Every saint,' worthy or unworthy, was to receive the same salutation. The spirit of Christian brotherhood was to prevail. **In Christ Jesus**—that is, with a Christian salutation. **The brethren that are with me greet you.** These are probably the more intimate companions of the apostle, while "all the saints," in the next verse, embraces the wider circle of the entire church at Rome. Who these brethren were, we do not know. There is no reason for the change of the verb from 'salute' in the first sentence to 'greet' in the second, since it is the same verb and is correctly translated 'salute.'

22. He adds "another cluster" of salutations from the members of the church at Rome, and especially from the inmates of the imperial household. These last were probably the servants, as it was among the lower classes that the gospel first won a hearing (1 Cor. 1 : 26); and besides, had any of the emperor's relatives become Christians, history would undoubtedly have preserved some trace of the fact. Why the greeting from them was so emphasized, we cannot tell; but it may be that these Christians had ministered to Paul's necessities, and were very much moved by

23 The grace of our Lord Jesus Christ *be* with you all. Amen.

23 The grace of the Lord Jesus Christ be with your spirit.

the kindness of the distant Philippians to the lonely prisoner, and so sent their greeting with such affectionate earnestness as to reflect itself in his language. At any rate, a greeting from such a source was well worthy of special attention, for, as Calvin well says, "it is worthy of remark, as being no common instance of divine mercy, that the gospel had penetrated that abyss of all wickedness and debauchery—the imperial palace." Out of this reference grew the well-known legend of a correspondence between Paul and Seneca, Nero's preceptor.

23. The grace of our Lord Jesus Christ be with you all. The benediction is similar to that in Rom. 16 : 24; 1 Cor. 16 : 23; 1 Thess. 5 : 28; 2 Thess. 3 : 18; but especially to that in Gal. 6 : 18. The true reading is that of the Revised Version, *with your spirit*, which appears in Gal. 6 : 18; 2 Tim. 4 : 22 and Philem. 25 with very slight variations. The reading of the Common Version is more like Paul's usual benedictions, and which on that account probably crept in here through the error of some copyist. In every epistle this apostolic benediction was always written by Paul's own hand, and was "the token in every epistle" of its genuineness. See Col. 4 : 18; 2 Thess. 3 : 17.

www.ingramcontent.com/pod-product-compliance
Lightning Source LLC
Chambersburg PA
CBHW030718110426
42739CB00030B/740

* 9 7 8 3 3 3 7 7 3 1 0 5 2 *